Community Life
in the Early Church

Sheldon O. Juell

KOINONIA

P R E S S

PASADENA · CA

Community Life in the Early Church
Copyright © 1999
Sheldon Orville Juell

ISBN 0-9703255-0-9

To "my girl" Ivone

Thank you for your love, patience, support

and prayer which encouraged me

to complete this project.

I also dedicate this project

to my future children

who are being thought of at this time.

Thank you from the depths of my heart.

I LOVE YOU TEDDY BEAR!

Acknowledgments

I never dreamed that I could start and complete a project of this magnitude, but I did by the grace of God. I, first of all, want to thank my Lord and Savior Jesus Christ for His gracious gift of salvation that has been freely given to me, and the Holy Spirit who guided, directed and empowered me to complete this project. This project would not have been completed without the love and support of the following friends and relatives who contributed towards my spiritual, emotional, physical and academic formation:

- To God's greatest gift of love, my wife, Ivone who inspires and encourages me to be the person that God intends for me to be. I love you Teddy Bear!
- To my parents, Dr. Norman and Sharon Juell, who have always been there for me with their love, support, and prayer, who never gave up on me and continually told me that "you can do anything you put your mind to do." I love you both deeply!
- To my mother-in-law, Maria de Lourdes Garcia Demetrio, who demonstrates the love of God in and through her life daily and whose servant heart has had a tremendous impact upon my life.
- To my grandparents, Elmer and Mildred Juell and Orville and Marjorie Yingst, who have passed on to me their Christian heritage, and demonstrated the fruit of the Spirit in their lives as an example for me to follow.
- To David and Ivana Redmond for their continual love, support, and encouragement. Thank you for believing in my dreams and thus investing in my life and future.
- To my two brothers and their families: Clifton, Cheryl, Jason, Tyler and Ashleigh, and Lyndon and Courtney. I treasure your lives and I love you all very deeply.

Table of Contents

List of Tables

List of Figures

Forward

As a pastor in Los Angeles, I look about, observe hectic lifestyles and proceed to ask questions. Questions like, "How did we become so disjointed and disconnected?" How can we be surrounded by millions of people and be so lonely?" "Is it possible to build community in a commuter society?"

If death can be defined as "separation" then too many die little deaths daily. We deeply need resurrection life and resurrected relationships. Only Jesus can provide both—after all, He is the resurrection and the life. By knowing where to begin, we can then proceed to discover the key truths for reconnecting and re-establishing healthy relationships. This is where Sheldon Juell takes us in his book, *Community Life in the Early Church.*

Sheldon Juell has captured not only this quest for community but has also directed our attention to the origins of Kingdom connections as expressed in the early church. By taking us back to the beginning, we find out the whys and the hows of godly relationships. But Sheldon does not leave us in a time warp; he also presents practical applications for authentic community in our contemporary society.

Specifically, Sheldon identifies the heart of community—love—and also explains how the heartbeat of prayer and worship, in concert with the Holy Spirit, pumps life into the followers of Jesus. Are there obstacles to overcome? By all means, and here too Sheldon pulls back the layers to uncover the hidden dangers lurking beneath the surface to ruin and spoil the Lord's intentions for His people. Unity in the community does not happen by default but only through intentional obedience to the Master's Plan. Are there risks involved? Of course, but the vision provided and insights offered invite each of us to count the cost and invest in such a way as to build lasting relationships. After all, why not experience a little bit of heaven now by living according to heaven's priorities?

Perhaps the most challenging segment of the book deals with church leadership. I live in the entertainment capitol of the world and am inundated by high profile personalities who wield worldwide influence. We live in an age that prizes style more than substance and image more than content. As a result, it is easy to become captured by the spirit of this age. Here Sheldon not only challenges leadership to think differently, but to return to God's original intentions for leaders. As we do, we find liberty and liberality, direction and directives.

When I read Sheldon's manuscript, I wasn't surprised. After all, he and I have talked often about these internal stirrings bubbling up from within his soul. He has not dabbled into abstract theory but has delved into the practical inner workings of the church as it was intended to work. And you guessed it, it only works well when we are well connected to Jesus and to one another in love. Enjoy, and let the words soak deeply and let them probe where they will.

Pastor Ed Stanton
Angelus Temple
Los Angeles, California

Preface

This purpose of this book is to examine the pattern of community life that existed in the Early Church. It suggests how the contemporary Church can model this pattern in today's society. The Church must reevaluate how the world sees and responds to Her and unite as one body under the power and anointing of the Holy Spirit in order to once again be effective witnesses in our communities like the Early Church. In order to accomplish this task the Church must become and function as one like the Community of Love is and functions as one (Jn. 17:1-26).

Our highest calling is to reflect the unity of this heavenly community. The church today has become an enemy to the sinner, and not a hospital for sinners, where the hurting, the hopeless, the discouraged, the depressed, and the confused can find love, acceptance, and forgiveness. Jesus brought healing to the whole person! Likewise, Jesus has called us to be His instruments through the ministry of the Holy Spirit in the communities in which we live. Jesus has called us to be His body incarnate and bring His salvation to our world. The Church today must come to the realization that "the church is only the church when it exists for others" (Giles 1995:12).

The fellowship of the Early Church only had meaning as it ministered in the world. On the one hand, unless the church is in the world it ceases to be the church—the body of Christ. On the other hand, as C. René Padilla states "The church must be in the world; the world must not be in the church" (1985:46). We have allowed worldly influences to condition the Church even to the degree that it shapes the message and methods of the gospel of Jesus Christ. This must stop! It is not enough just to fellowship with other believers. The essence of this fellowship is seen only as we—the body of Christ—are active in the world as ambassadors of the Community of Love.

Pasadena   Sheldon O. Juell
California   January 2001

Introduction

The greatest need in the world today is love, acceptance, and forgiveness. Whether believer or nonbeliever, people need to know that they are unconditionally loved, accepted, and forgiven. These terms are necessary if there is to be a community of God that will attract others into this lifestyle. This book is the result of a personal struggle for the body of Christ to respond to other members who are also a part of this same community, but feel neglected. Often I have felt that I am alone in this battle and when I reach out for the help of other Christians, it seems as though they are turning their back to me. I believe that there are many other Christians who are going through this same struggle and cannot find anyone to help them cope with these daily struggles.

We as the body of Christ must come to the reality that we are not functioning as God the Father, God the Son, and God the Holy Spirit intended for us to function. Their intention is for Their body to function as a community since we are created to live in community like They live in community. In the day in which we live, there is an ever-increasing focus on churches competing with each other. This is often seen in the leadership of one church trying to supercede the evangelistic efforts of a neighboring church and instead they should be working together. It is also seen in members of one denomination attacking another because of their doctrines and becoming closed-minded to the beliefs of another denomination. It is time for the body of Christ to recognize their beliefs and the beliefs of others and join together in one accord so that the Gospel may go forth in the power of the Holy Spirit. Denominationalism since its beginning has divided the body of Christ and caused us to live contrary to how we were created to live, as a community.

The greatest example of this is exemplified in the Early Church, which was a united force under the direction of the Holy Spirit. The key to the spread of the gospel was the power of the Holy Spirit operating within the lives of its members. Within one generation the gospel had been spread throughout

1

the known world. However, in the day in which we live, this powerful force is being neglected because we think that we can "go into all the world and preach the good news to all creation" (Mk. 16:15) in our own strength and as a result we are failing miserably. It is only as we unite under the power and anointing of the Holy Spirit that these existing barriers between one church and another, one denomination and another will be broken down.

The greatest need in the world today is love, acceptance, forgiveness. Whether believer or nonbeliever, people need to know that they are unconditionally loved, accepted, and forgiven.

Then, like the Early Church, we will be able to reach our known world with the gospel as a unified body of believers.

It is time for the body of Christ to understand and return to the original design that God intended for His people to function, grow and mature together and not try to do it on our own strength. Before the body of Christ can become the community that God designed us to be, we need to first of all deal with our lack maturity in the Lord which will lead to unity and ultimately community.

Today, it is common to hear about gay people who are coming out of the closet and confessing who they think they are, and also those who are living a promiscuous lifestyle. It is time for the body of Christ to come out of the closet, and let the world know who we are in Christ, stand up for what we believe, and take back what the enemy has stolen. The purpose of this book is to describe the Early Church as the necessary model that the church Jesus inaugurated must follow if it will once again be the church that it already is. God created a community in the beginning, patterned after the Community of Love that exists between the Father, Son, and Holy Spirit, to function corporately and to relate to others as true brothers and sisters in the Lord. The focus of this book will be limited to the 1st century church, particularly the foundation of the church in the first three decades (4 B.C. to 30 A.D.).

Even though there are great men and women theologians who have written about community, this book will utilize primarily the Word of God to convey the community life of the Early Church. The Early Church was founded upon Jesus Christ, and the scriptures that were available to them. The world around us is crying for freedom and we have been gifted by God to take His message of salvation, freedom, healing, deliverance, restoration, reconciliation, and wholeness to our known world. Please hear my heart as you read, but even more than that, take the principles that are presented and make a difference in the community in which you live.

"You know the message God sent to the people of Israel, telling the good news of peace through Jesus Christ, who is Lord of all. You know what has happened throughout Judea, beginning in Galilee after the baptism that John preached—how God anointed Jesus of Nazareth with the Holy Spirit and power, and how he went around doing good and healing all who were under the power of the devil, because God was with him" (Acts 10:36-38).

"The Spirit of the Lord is on me, because he has anointed me to preach good news to the poor. He has sent me to proclaim freedom for the prisoners and recovery of sight for the blind, to release the oppressed, to proclaim the year of the Lord's favor" (Lk. 4:18-19).

"But you will receive power when the Holy Spirit comes on you; and you will be my witnesses in Jerusalem, and in all Judea and Samaria, and to the ends of the earth" (Acts 1:8).

Chapter 1

Background to the Early Church

The purpose of this chapter is to describe the geographical, historical, cultural, sociological and economic background in which the Early Church was established. It is literally impossible to study any subject without a good understanding of its history. To do so would be like painting a picture without perspective. This chapter sets the foundation on which the remainder of this book builds upon and paints a picture of early first century life.

"I rejoiced with those who said to me, 'Let us go to the house of the Lord.' Our feet are standing in your gates, O Jerusalem. Jerusalem is built like a city that is closely compacted together. That is where the tribes go up, the tribes of the Lord, to praise the name of the Lord according to the statute given to Israel. There the thrones for judgment stand, the thrones of the house of David. Pray for the peace of Jerusalem: 'May those who love you be secure. May there be peace within your walls and security within your citadels.' For the sake of my brothers and friends, I will say, 'Peace be within you.' For the sake of the house of the Lord our God, I will seek your prosperity" (Ps. 122:1-9).

The psalmist states that the house of the Lord should be a place where each believer experiences intimacy with the Lord with a joyful heart, fellowship with the Holy Spirit and the love, acceptance, and forgiveness of other believers. Psalms 122 presents

This is the nation's rallying-point, where scattered tribes are enclosed in the unity of one worship and one law; it is the seat of justice and government, and above all, the national shrine. Patriotism, piety, and the sense of the unity of God's people from many places, combine in prayer for the city's peace and prosperity (Elwell 1989:394).

4

Geographical Background to the Early Church

It is very important in the study of the Early Church to describe the geographical background, which provides the necessary milieu into the establishment of the Early Church.

The Origin of the City of Jerusalem

Many scholars and Rabbis have agreed that the origin of the name of Jerusalem commonly signifies, "a foundation," "the abode," or "the inheritance of peace." "They make it a compound of *Jireh* and *Shalem*, and say that Abraham called it 'Jehovah-Jireh,' while Shem had named it *Shalem*, but that God combined the two into Jireh-Shalem, Jerushalaim, or Jerusalem" (Edersheim 1950:25).

According to other scholars the name Jerusalem also signifies "possession of peace," "constitution of harmony," "vision of peace," and "abode of prosperity." The first part of Jerusalem, *Jeru* means "founding," "constituting," while the second part *Salem* means "peace," "quiet," "safety," "harmony," "prosperity."

Jerusalem was to be the city that founded or constituted a community of peace, harmony, and prosperity; a place that established a new community, something that had long been sought after and now was being created. The name *Salem* described "the foundation of (the god) *Shalem*," "the patron-god of the city," or "the city of *Shalem*." Therefore, there was a particular holiness ascribed to Jerusalem before King David began to rule (Elwell 1996:392). The city of Jerusalem[1] is first referenced in Joshua 10:1, and the last is in Revelation 21:2, and

---

[1] "Jerusalem, formerly called Jebus (Judg. 19:10), was a stronghold of the Jebusites, one of the seven nations that the Israelites were to drive out of the land (3:10). The king and his army were annihilated by Joshua and Israel, the city itself remained uncaptured until after Joshua's death (Judg. 1:8). Some years later it was captured again and became the royal city (2 Sam. 5:6-9)" (Gaebelein 1992, 3:301).

is described symbolically as the redeemed state of humankind. The authors of the *Metaphysical Bible Dictionary* beautifully state that the heart of Jerusalem,

> In man it is the abiding consciousness of spiritual peace, which is the result of continuous realizations of spiritual power tempered with spiritual poise and confidence. Jerusalem is the "city of David," which symbolizes the great nerve center just back of the heart. From this point [the] Spirit sends its radiance to all parts of the body (1962:341-342).

This captures the essence of the Jerusalem as the "habitation of peace," the spinal cord of the Christian faith and the body of Christ. It describes the life-flow of God through the Holy Spirit to give energy and radiance to the rest of the body. This same Spirit would be responsible for the outpouring of the Holy Spirit on the Day of Pentecost and the giving of gifts to each member of the body of Christ (1 Cor. 12:11).

Jerusalem's Topography

The importance of Jerusalem is not the result of natural endowments except for a perennial spring. Jerusalem consists of two ridges (eastern and western) and its limestone plateau is 800 meters above sea level in the central hill country, which borders on the Judean desert, and some distance from the major trade routes. Its land is agriculturally poor with an arid climate and has a limestone base is devoid of valuable minerals. Strabo, a Greek geographer of the first century A.D. described Jerusalem as a place that would not be envied, or a place where one would fight (Achtemeier 1985:463).

Jerusalem is situated on a rugged terrain with the Judean mountains to the west, Judean desert and descends to the Dead Sea to the east. This strategic location had military benefits, and was easy to defend due to this terrain. However, Jerusalem was not an important natural commercial center. Its location and natural features were a commercial drawback, because the commercial centers of Palestine were located on the coastal plain and not on these two ridges. It did not straddle a major trade crossroad like Shechem or Bethel. These eastern ridges, include the part of the north by the Kidron Valley, and on the west and south by the Hinnon Valley. Josephus describes a small north-south valley known as the Tyropoeon Valley, which is only a slight depression today. It was also known as the Central Valley or in biblical terms "the valley" (Freedman 1992, 3:751).

Jerusalem was not blessed with an abundant water supply. The primary water supply was the Spring Gihon, and was also known as the Virgin's Fountain, and located in the Kidron Valley and not naturally a protected site. A second spring, En-rogel, located in the middle of the Kidron but south of the city was even more exposed. The Gihon Spring was described as the remnant of one of the rivers of Eden (Gen. 2:13). Mount Moriah, the Temple Mount, was seen as the foundation or navel of the earth. Overall, Jerusalem, was not a well-designed city (Achtemeier 1985:463).

Jerusalem was to the Jews "the city the Lord had chosen out of all the tribes of Israel in which to put his Name" (1 Kgs. 14:21); to the Christians it is the place where Jesus was crucified, buried and rose from the dead; to the Moslems it is the setting for Mohammed's visionary ascent to heaven (Quran 17:1) (Miller and Miller 1973:314). However, God has transformed this earthly Jerusalem, the dwelling place of God, into "the heavenly Jerusalem," the true sanctuary of the Lord (Heb. 12:22-29).

Historical Background to the Early Church

The historical background of the Early Church not only involved the Jews, but also the Greek and Roman contributions aided its historical development. God has taken these three primary contributions to make the greatest impact upon the establishment of the advent of Jesus. These contributions aided in impacting history in a way not possible before or since the time of Jesus' birth. The development of the historical data that surrounded the Early Church is a vital foundational stone in which to build a proper view of this period in history. This foundational stone is Jesus Christ (Eph. 2:18-22; 1 Pet. 2:4-8).

"Consequently, you are no longer foreigners and aliens, but fellow citizens with God's people and members of God's household, built on the foundation of the apostles and prophets, with Christ Jesus himself as the chief cornerstone. In him the whole building is joined together and rises to become a holy temple in the Lord. And in him you too are being built together to become a dwelling in which God lives by his Spirit" (Eph. 2:18-22).

Greek Influence on Christianity

Even though Rome politically conquered the Greeks, it was the Greeks who culturally conquered the Romans. It was Athens that provided a philosophical environment for the propagation of the gospel. The background in which Christianity developed can be traced is that of the Conquest of Palestine, and most of the known world, by Alexander the Great towards the last half of the fourth century B.C.

Alexander the Great[2] was a Macedonian soldier who greatly influenced the known world with the spirit and culture of the

---

[2] "Alexander the Great was born in Pella, Macedonia in 356 BC, to Philip II and Olympias (daughter of King Neoptolemus of Epirus), and died June 13, 323 in Babylon. From the age of 13 until 16 years of age he was taught by Aristotle in philosophy, medicine, and scientific research, and later advanced beyond Aristotle's narrow understanding that non-Greeks should be treated as slaves. He conquered the Macedonian throne in 336 BC, and liquidated potential rivals, and consolidated his political power in Greece. Alexander the Great is recognized as one of the greatest generals in history, since he overthrew the Persian Empire, carried Macedonian arms to India, and established the foundation for the Hellenistic world of territorial kingdoms. Through all of his conquests and accomplishments, he became a legendary hero. The Macedonians were extravagant in their joys, fights, drinking, and sorrows" (Ferguson 1993:10-14).

Greeks. This spirit of the Greeks included an intense love for truth, an all-encompassing vision, and a bold and daring initiative. Palestine was ruled for almost two centuries after the death of Alexander the Great (Baker 1959:2).

The contributions of the Greek culture to the Christian movement are threefold: first, Greek philosophy, whether positive or negative, was scattered through the known world, prepared the way for the coming of Jesus Christ. Their philosophy was atheistic and skeptical, and negatively influenced the Gentile world. This influence turned many of the Gentiles from the superstitious worship of false gods and created an unquenchable hunger to know the one, true God. However, Greek philosophy had a positive influence because it enhanced the worth and value of the human spirit through their high regard for spiritual and moral truth (Baker 1959:3). Greek philosophy also destroyed the older religions.

> Whoever came to know its tenets, whether Greek or Roman, soon found that this intellectual discipline made his polytheistic religion so rationally unintelligible that he turned away from it to philosophy. But philosophy failed to satisfy his spiritual needs; so he either became a skeptic or sought comfort in the mystery religions of the Roman Empire (Cairns 1996:43).

By the time of Jesus' birth, philosophy had declined from the height that Plato had reached to a system of self-centered individualism adhered to various groups such as the Stoics[3] and

---

[3] "Stoic philosophy was founded by Zeno (335-263 BC) a native of Cyprus. It was based on a belief that both the world and its people ultimately depend on just one principle: 'Reason.' Since the world itself operates by this standard, men and women who want a good life must 'live in harmony with nature.' They could do this primarily through following their conscience, for that itself was also inspired by 'Reason.' This was something people could only do for themselves, and Stoics laid great emphasis on living a life of 'self-sufficiency.' Many of them were widely respected for their high standards of personal morality. It was not uncommon for them to be prepared to commit suicide sooner than lose their self-respect and dignity" (Drane 1992:19).

Epicureans.[4] Their philosophy viewed God as impersonal and detached from His creation, and could never present a personal God of love. The affect of this philosophy upon its adherents influenced them to view life spiritually, and left them empty, which only Jesus promised and was able to fill.

The Greek philosophers called their people to a reality that transcended the temporal and relative world in which they lived and functioned on a daily basis. Both Socrates and Plato (5th century) taught that the temporal world is only a glimpse of the real world whose ideals were that of the good, the beautiful and the true. They argued that reality was not of temporal and material origin, but of spiritual and eternal. To them truth never resulted in a personal relationship with God, but that the ultimate end of man seeking the true God was through their intellect. On the other hand, "Christianity offered to those who accepted Socrates' and Plato's philosophy the historical revelation of the good, the beautiful, and the true in the person of the God-man, Christ" (Cairns 1996:43).

There were other philosophies that influenced Christianity such as: first, the Cynics who viewed the supreme virtue as being simplistic and lived rejecting comfort, affluence, and social prestige; second, the Skeptics who were relativists rejected any belief that was absolute and yielded to doubt and conformity and prevailing custom. Even though these and other philosophies did not greatly influence the people, superstition and syncretism affected the masses. Therefore, when

---

[4] "Epicurean philosophy was founded by Epicurus (341-270 BC). Epicureans adopted a totally different view of life. Though many Greeks had debated what happens at death, they would have none of it. Death is the end, they said, and the only real way to make sense of life is to be detached as possible from it. A good life consists in 'pleasure.' For Epicurus, this means things like friendship and peace of mind. But many of his followers interpreted it differently, and gained a reputation for reckless living. There were other philosophical groups in New Testament times, however, they never appealed to the ordinary person. These philosophies were seldom able to stem the fears of the working classes. It was too time consuming to organize one's way of life this way" (Drane 1992:20).

Christianity came into being, it had to face a religiously and philosophically confused world. The traditional religions had not supplied the necessary answers to life and people felt helpless, without any hope and seeking a way of life, which would give them hope. The atmosphere at the advent of Jesus Christ was of gloom and despair (Gundry 1994:61). God's timing is perfect!

Second, Greek became the universal language spoke in the known world and by the time of Roman Empire most cultured Romans could read, write, and speak both Greek and Latin. The dialect of Athens (classical Greek), also spoken by Alexander the Great, his army, and merchants of the Hellenistic world between 338 and 146 B.C., was modified and spread throughout the Mediterranean world. This modified Greek was known as Koine Greek and became the common language of man. It was through Koine Greek that the early Christians were able to communicate with the peoples of the ancient world and enabled them to write the Greek New Testament. It also aided the Jews of Alexandria in the writing of the Old Testament in Koine Greek, known as the Septuagint. A German theologian stated, "the Greek of the New Testament was a special Greek given by the Holy Spirit for the writing of the New Testament" (Cairns 1996:42). Throughout Palestine, the Jews were obligated to learn Koine Greek so that they could function within society.

Third, the Greeks also made a valuable contribution to the religious practices of the known world to accept Christianity when it appeared. The institution of materialistic philosophy of the Greeks (6th century) brought a drastic end to the faith of the Greeks and their old polytheistic worship. Even though some characteristics of their worship remained mechanical, it soon lost its influence upon the Greek culture. "Philosophy became a system of pragmatic individualism under the successors of the Sophists or a system of pragmatic individualism, such as seen in the teachings of Zeno the Stoic and Epicurus" (Cairns 1996:44). Everett Ferguson states,

The conquests of Alexander effectively broadened the concept of the world and at the same time broke down the sense of security within the narrow confines of the old city-state. In the fourth century especially, the traditional religion, morality, and the way of life no longer seemed to be assured by the customs of a close-knit community. Many persons were looking for new foundations of conduct and a new sense of community. Individuals were on their own (1993:305).

These Hellenistic philosophers used their skills and reasoning to simply fill the needs of the Greeks, which only left a void that needed to be filled with something or someone substantial. This void could be filled at the advent of Jesus Christ. Their skills and reasoning were based upon Socrates' philosophy that one's soul is intellectual and moral personality and that man's primary function was to develop his own soul.

Therefore, both Greek and Roman philosophy contributed to the institution of Christianity through the destruction of old polytheistic religions and by proving the inability of human reason or philosophical persuasions as being sufficient to reach God. This led people to think in terms of sin and redemption, which made Christianity more receptive within the Roman Empire since it offered a spiritual approach to life.

Roman Influence on Christianity

The Roman period began with the founding of Rome in the 8th century B.C. The primary contribution of the Romans was political. Even though the Romans were idolatrous and followed the practices of mystery religions and emperor worship, they were used by God, of whom they did not know, to fulfill His will through them. Historically, Greek dominance over Palestine ended about 165 B.C. when Judas Maccabeus and his Jewish soldiers defeated the Greeks. In 63 B.C. after Jewish independence, which lasted about a century, Roman soldiers conquered Palestine (Baker 1959:4).

The New Testament is full of references to Roman rule. There is evidence to Roman centurions (Mt. 8:8), Roman guards (Mt. 28:11), Roman jailers (Acts 16:33), Roman citizens (Acts 16:37), Roman castles, and governors. The Pharisees tried to trap Jesus when they asked Him concerning whether Jews should serve God or Roman rule (Mt. 22:15-22). Matthew was an unpopular publican because he collected taxes for Rome (Mt. 9:9-13).

Roman rule at the time of Christ was not completely positive or completely negative in its effect upon Christianity. Positively, Roman rule was a strong centralized government, which provided its citizens with peace and protection. Its government would not allow any type of riot or violence to occur with its empire because it might cause a political revolt. This type of government made the expansion of the gospel among the various ethnic groups within the Mediterranean world with little or no political hindrance. Roman citizens like the apostle Paul were protected from unjust punishment at the hands of local officials.

Negatively, Roman government became Christianity's greatest enemy by the end of the first century. The Roman mindset of this time had little understanding of the worth of a person's soul, choosing rather to devote themselves fully to the service of the state. As Roman rule conquered every nation they would adopt its false gods, and required that each conquered nation worship Roman gods, including the Roman emperor. However, when Christians refused to bow and worship Roman gods and its emperor, they were severely persecuted (Baker 1959:4). The influence of the Roman Empire was tremendous and extended in every direction from Rome. At the time when the New Testament was being written the entire known world, except some kingdoms in the Far East, was under the rule of the Roman Empire.

From the Atlantic Ocean on the west to the Euphrates River and the Red Sea on the east, and from the Rhone, the Danube, the Black Sea and the Caucasus mountains on the north to the Sahara on the south, there stretched one vast empire under the headship and virtual dictatorship of the emperor, called in the New Testament both "king" (1 Pet. 2:17) and "Augustus" (Luke 2:1) in the New Testament (Tenney 1985:3).

The Romans were unique in that they developed a unity among humankind under a universal law, which in turn created a favorable climate for the expansion of the gospel. Rome, like no other empire even that of Alexander the Great, was successful in uniting humankind together in a political organization. This type of political organization was customary among the citizens of the Roman Empire. Unity within the Roman Empire grew even more when non-Romans, those within the Mediterranean world, were allowed to become citizens, and placed everyone under the rule of one system and citizenship of one kingdom. Therefore, this universal law unified all humankind, stating that all were born under the penalty of sin and in need of a Savior who would place them within a universal community called the body of Christ (Cairns 1996:39-40).

God, through adversity and captivity instilled two profound truths into their hearts: the first was "Hear, O Israel: The Lord our God, the Lord is one" (Dt. 6:4); *second, the relationship between God and man is personal and not national.*

The Romans had many conquests, which lead to unbelief among various ethnic groups because their gods were not powerful enough to save them from the Roman defeat. This left these ethnic groups in a spiritual vacuum with no hope of complete satisfaction from the religions of the day. Rome's substitute for the gods only enhanced their need for a more spiritual faith. Our sovereign and omniscient God had His hand upon the development and institution of the Roman Empire, which culminated each part of history to introduce humankind to our Lord and Savior Jesus Christ.

Jewish Influence on Christianity

The Jews influenced Christianity the most of these three races. However, great may have been the contributions of Athens and Rome to Christianity

> By way of environment, the contributions of the Jews stand forth as the *heredity* of Christianity. Christianity may have developed in the political milieu of Rome and may have had to face the intellectual environment created by the Greek mind, but its relationship to Judaism was much more intimate. Judaism may be thought as the stalk on which the rose of Christianity was to bloom (Cairns 1996:44).

The Jews provided the immediate background to the Early Church and the advent of Jesus Christ. God in His infinite wisdom chose a Jewish lineage, which would become a nation. First of all, several factors contributed to the political division of 975 B.C. The Northern Kingdom fell into Assyrian captivity about 722 B.C. and the Southern Kingdom remained until it fell to the Babylonians about 587 B.C. After seventy years had passed remnants of the Southern Kingdom were set free and returned to Palestine, and remained subject to the Persians until Alexander the Great conquered them about 334 B.C. The Greek era (334-167 B.C.), the century of Jewish independence (167-63 B.C.), and the establishment of the Roman Empire (63 B.C.) brought the history of the Jews to the commencement of the New Testament era (Baker 1959:5).

As with the Romans and Greeks, the Jews were also unconsciously preparing the way for the advent of Jesus Christ. God, through adversity and captivity instilled two profound truths into their hearts: the first was "Hear, O Israel: The Lord our God, the Lord is one" (Dt. 6:4); second, the relationship between God and man is personal and not national. Before the Jews had fallen into the Babylonian captivity, they would worship idols and were polytheistic, however, when they returned from captivity to Palestine they became zealous for the things of God, teaching the truth that God is one (monotheistic). While in Palestine, the Jews fell back on their former way of life; however, they had learned their lesson in Babylon, remembering that the individual must commune with God through the Holy Spirit (Baker 1959:5).

The beliefs and practices of the Jews were well known throughout the known world. During the initial beginnings of the Greek period, a movement known as the Dispersion, scattered Jews from Palestine throughout the Mediterranean world. Wherever the Jews were scattered they proselytized many and established synagogues to continue their belief and practices. They longed for the return of their Messiah, and prepared everyone for this event (Cairns 1996:44).

The Jews, unlike the Greeks, did not rely upon human reason in their discovery of God. God had revealed Himself in history through Abraham and others, and through the captivities they had learned of the existence of God and without hesitation worshipped Him because He is worthy. Jerusalem became the representative and foundation for which Christianity could be established, as Jesus told the Samaritan woman at the well "for salvation is from the Jews" (Jn. 4:22). From this small nation strategically situated at the crossroads of Africa, Europe and Asia, the Lord and Savior of humankind would begin His ministry to "to seek and to save what was lost" (Lk. 19:10).

Cultural Background to the Early Church

There existed many tensions between the cultures of the Early Church. This cultural world was a turmoil of confusing and conflicting cultures. The various countries and cultures of the Mediterranean world, which was in constant expansion through Rome, all contributed to the cultural milieu of Christianity. The association of social and religious forces that had been brought together under Rome created a unique setting for the birth of Christianity. All of these theological and philosophical differences influenced and affected the interpretation of the gospel (Tenney 1965:67). The countries listed in Acts 2:9-11,[5] all had a considerable Jewish population within its borders, seem to be listed in linguistic categories, which alludes to emphasizing that the gospel transcends linguistic barriers (Kistemaker 1990:82).

The three prevalent cultures at this time were Judaism, Hellenism, and Roman imperialism.

Judaism provided the roots of Christianity; Hellenism, the intellectual soil in which it grew; and imperialism, the protection that opened the field of its growth. Paradoxically, these three cultures became Christianity's bitterest enemies, for Judaism regarded it as a pernicious heresy, Hellenism as philosophical nonsense, and Roman imperialism as impractical weakness (Tenney 1965:67).

Even though each of these three conflicted with the other two in ancestry and worldview, they established the foundation for the Early Church.

Judaism

Even though they were dispersed from their homeland, they continued their religious and cultural customs, which distinguished them from others. They remained unified in their observance of Jewish customs, while adapting themselves to their new environment, language, and dress. They never really adhered to the Roman way of life. Some of these Jewish colonies were large as in Alexandria and Antioch, while others were relatively small, as in Philippi, because there were not enough members to constitute a Synagogue (Acts 16:13, 16).

---

5 "Parthians, Medes and Elamites; residents of Mesopotamia, Judea and Cappadocia, Pontus and Asia, Phrygia and Pamphylia, Egypt and the parts of Libya near Cyrene; visitors from Rome (both Jews and converts to Judaism); Cretans and Arabs—we hear them declaring the wonders of God in our own tongues!" (Acts 2:9-11).

No matter their location, the Jews always established a resistance to polytheism and their rituals were spread throughout the land. Although Judaism can be interpreted as a strict adherence to the rituals of the Jerusalem Temple or by the Samaritans and Hellenists who were indifferent to these Temple rituals, it paved the way for the gospel.

The Jewish culture differed greatly from that of the Greek culture. The primary difference was in their mental attitude and religion, which was directly by the Law and the development of the principles in the Torah.

The Greek maintained a spirit of free inquiry stimulated by an insatiable intellectual curiosity which impelled him to probe all aspects of the world and to offer new hypothesis concerning its nature and laws. The Jews were religious, the Greeks, scientific in their outlook; and despite mutual tolerance, they never found a lasting union of faith (Tenney 1965:71).

Hellenism

The Greeks and Romans differed slightly in their religious preferences; they united together under the mentality that characterized the Roman Empire. The civil wars that occurred two centuries before the advent of Christ left them without resources and stability and its people desperately longing for peace and hope. Hellenistic influence was not based on political sovereignty, but on the influence of its ideas and lure of its culture.

Hellenistic thought influenced most of the New Testament and the mindset of the earliest members of the Early Church. Eleven out of the twelve disciples were from the area surrounding the Sea of Galilee, and understood the Greek language and customs. This was largely based on the fact that they were in constant contact with Gentiles who had immigrated from the West. The Jewish Dispersion contributed to a Hellenistic paradigm shift. They lived in constant tension and were forced to adjust to their Greek surroundings if they were to prosper. This pressure influenced them greatly and many of them changed their Jewish names and rituals and became Hellenized, but remained faithful to God (Tenney 1965:73).

Roman Imperialism

Even though the Roman culture was inferior and dependent upon the Greeks, they did not imitate them completely. First, in literature, Latin became the language used by lawyers and theologians because of it clear pattern of thought and definiteness; Greek was used by philosophers, historians, artists, and merchants. Second, Roman sculpture was more realistic and rugged than that of the Greeks whose sculpture was proportionately balanced and ideal. Third, the Romans were superior to others in engineering. The Roman baths, roads that still exist today, and architecture, set a precedent unsurpassed by any other culture. Fourth, they were known for their efficiency and resourcefulness, which became a vital part of Early Church procedures.

The warring cultures found a common ground in Christ. No outward change was visible in the faces, practices, or dress of the Christians, yet there was a perceptible alteration in their behavior, for they begun to build a culture of their own almost as soon as they professed conversion. Hebrew theology, Greek speculative thinking, and Roman jurisprudence united in the new society, which the gospel created (Tenney 1965:78).

Sociological Background to the Early Church

Jerusalem at the time of Christ, existed as a socially and culturally pluralistic urban center. Typical ancient cities included the rich, who were generally craftsmen, and the poor or destitute.

Jewish Society

The social world of the 1st century had many similarities compared to today's society. In Judaism there existed a wealthy aristocracy and social classes. The aristocracy primarily consisted of the families of the priesthood and leading rabbis. The rich and the poor, righteous men and criminals, freemen and slaves lived side by side, somewhat like our society today. Alfred Edersheim states,

> It may be safely asserted, that the grand distinction, which divided all mankind into Jews and Gentiles, was not only religious, but also social. However near the cities of the heathen to those of Israel, however frequent and close the intercourse between the two parties, no one could have entered a Jewish town or village without feeling, so to speak, in quite another world. The aspect of the streets, the building and arrangement of the houses, the municipal and religious rule, the manners and customs of the people, their habits and ways—above all, the family life, stood in marked contrast to what would be seen elsewhere. On every side there was evidence that religion here was not merely a creed, nor a set of observances, but that it pervaded every relationship, and dominated every phase of life (1876:86).

The Aristocracy

The primary form of government of Israel at this time was theocracy, which placed the High Priest as the representative of the people. This gave him the highest authority among the people and the nation. These High Priests, because of their position, were the most significant class, and therefore, the wealthiest. This wealth was not the result of the giving of tithes because many of the peasants did not always pay them due to their state of poverty (Jeremias 1969:148).

There existed an animosity between the wealthier priests and the poorer priests. During the time of Agrippa II, High Priestly families seemed to have sent their slaves to force the poor to pay their tithes, while the poorer priests suffered greatly

(Bauckham 1995:220). This High Priestly function was patterned after the Old Testament, however, when Jesus came, He established the priesthood of all believers.

Social Classes

Palestinian people were farmers, artisans, and few owned businesses, yet they were primarily poor. The idea of slavery within Judaism was not really practiced and most Palestinians were freemen. Some of Jesus' disciples such as: Simon Peter, his brother Andrew, James and John, sons of Zebedee, were fishermen who were businessmen and lived fairly well at their trade.

The social divisions of the Jews were hindered by their obligation to adhere to the Law. Since they were equally responsible and obedient to God and His ways, they were also to live moral and just lives as well. They believed in equal rights of all men. However, they saw a wealthy person as blessed by God's favor and righteous in His eyes, and all Jews could earn God's favor through good works. "While an aristocracy tends to be self-perpetuating, at least the inherent moral equality kept the Jewish oligarchy from becoming too oppressive" (Tenney 1985:49).

Music and the stage were committed to entertainment of the mob rather than stimulating the thought of intellectuals. The Roman stage degenerated rapidly and contributed directly to the moral degradation of the people. The farces and mimes of the early empire were coarse and cheap; their plots dealt with the lowest kind of life and their presentation was shameless (1985:53).

Pagan Society

In the pagan society of the 1st century, there was also a wealthy aristocracy. There were also social tensions that affected these new Christians, because Christianity was closely connected to Judaism. Jesus was a Jew, His disciples were primarily Jews, and everything He taught was founded upon Jewish Scriptures.

The Aristocracy

Unlike the Jewish society, the pagan world was sharply contrasted because the civil wars of Rome had disrupted the social life of the Roman Empire. Military service created certain social prestige and the favor or disfavor of the emperor directly affected social standing of most families. Social status was evident between the snobbery of the upper class and the indifference shown by the lower class. Ferguson states that there were two classes that existed within the aristocracy. The first or upper class was known as the senatorial order[6] and the second or lower class was known as the equestrian order.[7]

Many of these senatorial families had perished, though some had survived the civil wars of Rome (1993:52). The senatorial order and the equestrian order lead to a new aristocracy, which

---

[6] "In terms of birth and prestige the patricians represented the oldest nobility of Rome, ostensibly going back to the time of the kings. The roll of senatorial families was six hundred. There was a minimum property qualification of 250,000 denarii for admission to the senate. Membership in the senate was actually attained by filling one of the principle magistracies of Rome (quaestor, praetor, consul). The sign of senatorial standing was a broad purple stripe on the toga. . . . The senatorial class was important for providing the chief civilian and military administrators" (Ferguson 1993:53).

[7] "Their name is derived from earlier times when a man who could outfit his own horse for war was so named. They were known as knights and were a much larger group, with a property qualification of only 100,000 denarii. The political distinction from senators was not always social or even economic. The knights were often wealthy, educated, and related to senatorial families. A few sons of knights in each generation went into the senate, and those sons of senators who chose not to follow a political career became knights. Besides being born into the order, one could advance to the equestrian rank through acquiring wealth or through promotion in the army" (Ferguson 1993:53).

involved landholders, who controlled through influence the land or who tricked people who had become poor due to the wars to sell their land for a cheap price. They exploited every province that they conquered and reaped an enormous profit. This wealth weakened the aristocracy and discouraged the lower classes and through their hard work they prospered less each year (Tenney 1985:49).

Social Classes

The middle class, based on the rise of slavery and resulted from military captives, almost became extinct. Many of the middle class, had been killed in the wars and many others could not compete with slave labor, were eventually forced out from their land and estates and became dependent upon Rome for their sustenance. This type of social life was dangerous and unpredictable heavily influenced the Roman Empire. The poor could not hold a steady job and were considered worse than slaves, who at least had food shelter and clothing. The poor fell prey to anyone who could give them a better life.

Slavery

Slavery was a well-established part of the ancient society. It played a tremendous role in both the Hellenistic and Roman periods and many prisoners of the civil wars created an abundance of slaves, which lowered the price of slaves. However, the stability of the Roman Empire created a market for homebred slaves and a major source of income. Everett Ferguson states, "It is estimated that one in five of the residents of Rome was a slave. A proposal in the senate that slaves be required to wear a distinctive dress was defeated lest the slaves learn how numerous they were" (1993:56). Merrill C. Tenney, on the other hand, states

No exact figures are obtainable, but probably less than half of the inhabitants of the Roman world were free men, and only relatively few of them were citizens with full rights. War, debt, and birth recruited the ranks of the slave population at a rapid rate. Many were physicians, accountants, teachers, and skilled artisans of every kind. Epictetus, a renowned philosopher, was one of the them (1985:50).

Paul addressed the issue of slaves and their master and that there existed Christians who were slaves and slaveholders (Eph. 6:5-9; 1 Pet. 2:18-19). Paul stresses a reciprocal attitude to exist between slaves and masters. The slaves were commanded to obey their masters and the masters were commanded not to treat their slaves harshly or threaten them. Paul uses this analogy to describe the power of Christian fellowship, however, slavery gradually weakened, lost its impact and ceased to exist.

The Family in the Early Church

There are two words that are used to describe the family in the Early Church. The first is *patria*, which speaks of the family from a historical perspective. The second is οἶκος (*oikos*), which is much more common and describes the family as a household. In the Greco-Roman society, *oikos* was comparable to the Old Testament concept of *bet-ab*[8] or "father's house" (Freedman 1992, 2:768).

The family constituted the basic unit of society in all of the cultures that provides the background for the Early Church. In the New Testament the family is described as including a tribe

---

[8] "This was the third level of the kinship structure of Israel, and the one in which the individual Israelite felt the strongest sense of inclusion, identity, protection, and responsibility. The 'father's house' was an extended family, comprising all the descendants of a single living ancestor in a single lineage, excluding married daughters, male and female slaves, and their families, resident labors, and sometimes resident Levites" (Freedman 1992, 2:762).

or even a nation (Acts 3:25).[9] Although many factors contributed to the Jewish concept of family, erosion was the result of: (1) too many slaves, who trained the children rather being trained by their parents, disrupted the relationship between the parents and their children; (2) childlessness was seen as a major threat to marriage, which left the couple feeling chastised by God; (3) polygamy; (4) death of the husband; (5) rebellious children; (6) Sibling rivalry; and (7) adultery, was a serious threat and adulterers were punished swiftly and harshly (Packer, Tenney, and White 1995:416-419).

In the typical Greco-Roman family there existed a low birth rate, however, to encourage its citizens to have larger families, the government offered special allowances to families with more than three children. In the typical Palestinian family, it was common for a family to consist of many children. The nuclear and extended families would rejoice at the birth of a son, and were displeased when a daughter was born. As was their custom, a Jewish boy was circumcised on the eighth day and given a name, however, the naming of a daughter could take up to a month. Jewish families had no surnames: so a family and/or a person was distinguished from others by using the name of their father ("James the son of Zebedee," Mt. 4:21); those with a religious or political persuasion, they would use their name and religious sect ("Simon the Zealot," Mt. 10:4); their occupation ("Simon the tanner," Acts 10:6, 32); or their place of residence ("Joseph of Arimathea" Mk. 15:34) (Gundry 1994:49).

When a member of a family died, the entire surviving family would demonstrate affectionately types of behavior such as grief, tear their garments, fasting for days and even a few weeks, and hire professional mourners who were primarily

---

[9] "In Acts 3:25 the promise to Abraham is quoted in the form, 'in your posterity shall all the families (patriai) of the earth be blessed.' The LXX has 'tribes' (phylai) in the original promise (Gen. 12:3) and 'nations' (ethne) when the promise is recalled in Gen. 18:18 and 22:18" (Douglas 1962:371).

flutists and women skilled at wailing. Finally, the family would often request that an undertaker conduct the burial of their family member (Gundry 1994:49).

Marriage in the Early Church

The predominate form of marriage in the Jewish, Greek and Roman society was monogamous. Extramarital affairs were common, primarily in the Greek and Roman society, and prostitution and adultery readily available. Common law marriages constituted marriage in all societies with the primary reason to procreate. Each marriage was to be registered in order to make children legitimate. Daughters were generally married between the age of twelve to fifteen, and sons at an older age, approximately thirty for Greek men, and eighteen for Jewish men. Marriage was praised by Jewish religious teachers and was known as a normal part of the Jewish society. Frequently, these teachers would say, "He who has no wife lives without joy, blessing, or good" (Ferguson 1993:68).

Children in the Early Church

The primary fact concerning children was the high mortality rate. They were considered important for the security of the community and parents. To the Romans, children were vulnerable, and physically and mentally weak. Although puberty brought physical changes, the adolescent was seen as being able to reason and function like an adult. The main division between childhood and adulthood (the most important social event) was marriage for the daughter and registering as a citizen for the son (Ferguson 1993:68).

In the Greek family, it was rare to have more than three children, with a common household number of only one child. Families would often desire to have two sons in case one was killed and seldom would a family have more than one daughter since they were regarded as a liability. Infanticide was a sharp contrast between the Romans and Greeks and the Jews and Christians and was instituted to control the population. It was enforced by the parent leaving the unwanted child to die a horrific death in a pile of garbage or in some isolated place. Often these unwanted children were found by slave traders and/or prostitutes and raised in the same lifestyle (Ferguson 1993:73).

Morals of the Early Church

Sexual immorality was considered the primary prohibited act, and was attributed to the pagan gods and goddesses. Any form of immorality with "temple virgins" was seen as a vital part of the pagan religious rituals. It was very common for men and women to prostitute themselves, their spouse, and children. One of the most widely accepted forms of homosexual behavior was pederasty[10] along with other types of similar behavior. Marriage required a form of consent, then a withdrawal of consent by one or both parties made divorce quick, frequent, and acceptable to the Romans and Greeks. However, divorce to the Jews was the sole right of the husband (cf. Mk. 10:11-12 with Mt. 5:32) (Gundry 1994:50).

Economic Background to the Early Church

The economic life of the Early Church was no different than it is today. The proclamation and living out their faith on a daily basis was affected by the economic conditions. This subject is too extensive and too complex to adequately portray it properly, therefore, it will only be briefly discussed.

The primary basis of agricultural economy of the Mediterranean world was the olive tree, vine, grain, and sheep and its main food supply was the product of Egypt and Africa.

---

[10] "Lover of boys; one that practices anal intercourse especially with a boy" (Mish 1993:856).

The lack of technology greatly hindered the development of industry for mass production. However, there were traditional industries such as ceramics, mining (lead, silver, and iron), textiles (wool and silk), and various other handicrafts. During the Early Church era, glass blowing was invented, which surpassed the skill of glass making and provided an abundance of glass products. The marketplace was the center of activity in the Mediterranean world. Ferguson states,

> Mediterranean cities were built around the marketplace (Gk. *Agora*, Lat. *forum*). In those cities influenced by Hellenistic town-planning the marketplace was a large open area, rectangular in shape, given over to public monuments and statues. It was surrounded by a covered porch (*stoa*), which had shops and offices behind. Life then, as now, in Mediterranean countries was lived mostly outdoors, and the town marketplace was the center of life—a marketplace of conversation and ideas as well as of economic activities (cf. Acts 17:17) (1993:75).

The Care of the Poor

The welfare of each individual was the responsibility of the closest male known as the kinsman-redeemer. He was to "avenge his blood" and redeem his kinsman from indebtedness (Num. 35:12, 19; Lev. 24-26). During the Hellenistic and Roman periods there was a tremendous contrast between the wages paid to the poor and the generosity of the rich. The rich would give generously to public events and also respond generously to people's needs in a time of crisis, however, they refused to pay a generous wage to a hired worker (Ferguson 1993:75).

Economic Status within the Early Church

The Early Church had a good representation of the economic status of the people in Jerusalem. Many of its members were considered wealthy, even though there is no definite proof that they were among the wealthy elite. The Jerusalem church had members who were unselfish in their giving to the poor and needy (Acts 4:34-37). The faith of the members of the Early Church was affected by the prevailing economic conditions, which is no different than in today's churches.

The Upper Class

Some examples of the upper or elite class are: Simon of Cyrene, "the father of Alexander and Rufus, was passing by on his way in from the country" (Mk. 15:21), owned farm or estate near Jerusalem. Barnabas sold his property in Cyprus "sold a field he owned and brought the money and put it at the apostles' feet" (Acts 4:36f.). The well-known example of Ananias and Sapphira (Acts 5:1) also owned and "sold a piece of property . . . and put it at the apostles feet."

No definite reference is given to substantiate the size of these farms or estates, however, in the examples of Barnabas and Ananias the sale of their property was a significant sum of money. The Greek uses the word κτῆμα[11] to describe the size and worth of the property. Mary, the mother of John Mark, owned a large home that was used as a place of assembly for the Early Church (Acts 12:12).

The Lower Class

The lower class also had a good representation in the Early Church, which included some of Jesus' disciples. Zebedee, the father of James and John, owned a prosperous fishing business near Galilee and probably employed laborers. The trade of

---

[11] "Ktema is used in the Greek as a synonymous concept and means not only money, or goods and chattels which can be turned into money (Brown 1986, 2:844); it refers to a concrete possession, namely, a plot of land" (Balz and Schneider 1990, 2:324).

fishing and being a fisherman[12] is referred to both in the Old Testament (Isa. 19:8; Jer. 16:16, Eze. 47:10) and in the New Testament (Mt. 4:18-19; Mk. 1:16-17; Lk. 5:2; Jn. 21:7). At least seven of Jesus' disciples were fishermen: Peter and Andrew, probably Philip from Bethsaida ("house of fishing"), James, John, Thomas and Nathanael (Mt. 4:18, 21; Jn. 1:44; 21:2). James was one of the pillars of the Early Church and by trade was a carpenter like his brother Jesus (Gal. 1:19; 2:9; 1 Cor. 15:7; Acts 15:13-21; 21:17-25). Most of the members of the Early Church were craftsmen or owned small businesses. (Bauckham 1995:227).

The Submerged Class

This class also had a good representation and since Jesus and the apostles healed many beggars and people with diseases, they would become members of the Early Church. However, there had to have been other types of impoverished people who were taken care of by the Early Church (Acts 6:1; 2:44ff; 4:34).

---

[12] "Fishermen, then and now, formed a distinct class. The strenuousness of the work (Lk. 5:2-5) ruled out the weak and the indolent. They were crude in manner, rough in speech and in their treatment of others (Lk. 9:49, 54; Jn 18:10). The fishermen's exposure to all kinds of weather made them hardy and fearless. They were accustomed to bear with patience many trying circumstances. They often toiled for hours without success; yet they were always ready to try once more (Lk. 5:5; Jn. 21:3). Such men, when impelled by the same spirit of their master, became indeed 'fishers of men' (Mt. 4:19; Mk. 1:17; Lk. 5:10)" (Bromiley 1982, 2:309).

Chapter 2

The Community
of Love

The purpose of this chapter is to describe the community of love that exists between the Father, the Son, and the Holy Spirit and how this attitude of love should influence our relationship with others. It places the Godhead at the center of the community that was intended from the beginning of all things.

"For God so loved the world that he gave his one and only Son, that whoever believes in him shall not perish but have eternal life" (Jn. 3:16).

"Dear friends, let us love one another, for love comes from God. Everyone who loves has been born of God and knows God. Whoever does not love does not know God, because God is love. This is how God showed his love among us: He sent his one and only Son into the world that we might live through him. This is love: not that we loved God, but that he loved us and sent his Son as an atoning sacrifice for our sins. Dear friends, since God so loved us, we also ought to love one another. No one has ever seen God; but if we love one another, God lives in us and his love is made complete in us. We know that we live in him and he in us, because he has given us of his Spirit" (1 Jn. 4:7-13).

The apostle John begins by admonishing the community of believers to "love one another, for love comes from God." Love is the distinguishing attribute of our Creator God. Love in this passage refers not only to an attitude of love, but also the practice of love within

Through demonstrating love towards "one another," *we are in fact expressing the greatest act of God, within the Trinity and towards humankind, to* "one another."

the community. Through demonstrating love towards "one another," we are in fact expressing the greatest act of God, within the Trinity and towards humankind, to "one another."

The greatest expression of love that we can demonstrate is to "'Love the Lord your God with all your heart and with all your soul and with all your strength and with all your mind'; and, 'Love your neighbor as yourself'" (Lk. 10:27). Luke quotes from Deuteronomy 6:5 and Leviticus 19:18, and demonstrates that God desires community with His people and these indispensable commands connect them to Himself. By responding to His love with love, gratitude and loyalty, we enjoy a covenant relationship with Him. These two commands sum up the message of the Law and the prophets. As we "love one another," God not only lives within us, but His love is made complete in us.

From the beginning, God the Father, God the Son, and God the Holy Spirit existed as the community of love (Isa. 43:10). Within the Trinity, the Holy Spirit is the dynamic of love, expressed between God the Father and God the Son. Stanley J. Grenz states, "God's purpose is to bring glory to his own triune nature by establishing a reconciled creation in which humans reflect the reality of the Creator" (1994:628). We were created by God to live in a community of love and any attempt to live outside of this community means that we do not have true knowledge of God and that we are not an expression of His Divine nature to other believers and to the world.

> We are one people, therefore, because we are the company of those who the Spirit has already brought to share in the love between the Father and the Son. We truly are the community of love, a people bound together by the love present among us through the power of God's Spirit. As His people, we are called to reflect in the present the eternal dynamic of the triune God, that community which we will enjoy in the great eschatological fellowship on the renewed earth (Grenz 1994:630).

Created For Community

The aim of God in history is the creation of an all-inclusive community of loving persons, with himself included in that community as its prime sustainer and most glorious inhabitant. I believe that God is gathering just such a community in our day. It is a community that combines eschatology with social action, the transcendent Lordship of Jesus with the suffering servant Messiah. It is a community of cross and crown, of conflict and reconciliation, or courageous action and suffering love. It is a community empowered to attack evil in all its forms, overcoming it with good. It is a community buoyed up by the vision of Christ's everlasting rule, not only imminent on the horizon but already coming to birth in our midst (Foster 1992:254).

God created Adam and Eve so that they may enjoy community with each other as Father, Son, and Holy Spirit enjoy community. If man was complete in himself, there would be no need to create a companion for him, which would bring him out of isolation and towards completion. Therefore, since the Trinity is community, the fellowship that humans have between each other must reflect the fellowship shared within the Trinity.

Because God himself is triune, we are in the image of God only as we enjoy community with others. Only as we live in fellowship can we show forth what God is like. Ultimately, then, the "image of God" is a social reality. It refers to humans as beings-in-fellowship.

As we live in love—that is, as we give expression to true community—we reflect the love which characterizes the Creator himself. And as we reflect God's character which is love, we also live in accordance with our true nature. Only by being persons-in-community do we find our true identity—that form of the "world" toward which our "openness to the world," our restless shaping and reshaping of our environment, is intended to point us (Grenz 1996:79).

Jesus Himself expressed this truth to His disciples when He said, "If anyone would come after me, he must deny himself and take up his cross and follow me. For whoever wants to save his life will lose it, but whoever loses his life for me will find it" (Mt. 16:24-25). True life is the result of giving up one's life and living in community with Jesus and with others. Therefore, we can only find our true identity as we participate with other members in the community of love.

> But ultimately the enjoyment of fellowship is no mere private, individual experience. On the contrary, the fellowship God intends for us is a shared experience, and therefore, the divine image is likewise a shared, corporate reality. It is fully present only as we live in fellowship. It is ours only as we enjoy "community" (Grenz 1996:79).

As we work towards this end, we bring honor and glory to our Creator God through reflecting His nature, which is love. Our existence is the product of God's love, expressed through the eternal relationship of the Father and the Son, which is the Holy Spirit. Our Father desires that His

"God loves you just the way you are, but he refuses to leave you that way. He wants you to be just like Jesus."

creation share in His existence and enjoy the relationship that Jesus enjoys with the Father. Therefore, we are the product of God's love, and the world in which we live exists so that we may participate in the community life of the social Trinity. This theme of God establishing community with His creation is a central focus throughout Scripture.

> We are a sign likewise when we live as a community in the world. By being a true community of believers, we indicate what God intends for all mankind, namely, the establishment of the new community. Therefore, as we are a community in the world we implicitly call others to join us, to be reconciled and participate in God's community. Indeed, the gospel must be embodied—credibly demonstrated through our life together—if others are to see and acknowledge its truth. For this reason, truly being the presence of the community of Christ in the world is central to our evangelistic mission. And a vibrant fellowship of believers is one of our greatest apologetics for the truth of the gospel (Grenz 1996:223).

Created in the Image of Love

"Then God said, 'Let us make man in our image, in our likeness, and let them rule over the fish of the sea and the birds of the air, over the livestock, over all the earth, and over all the creatures that move along the ground.' So God created man in his own image, in the image of God he created him; male and female he created them" (Gen. 1:26-27).

When "God said, Let us make man in our image," the "image" He was emphasizing man's close similarity to Himself. As one looks in the mirror to see an image of themselves, "so God created man in his own image . . . male and female he created them." The phrase "in our likeness" refers to the fact that this similarity is not exact. God not only created us in the image of love, but He created us with a purpose. This purpose is to have rule or dominion over His creation; however, this dominion is based on the demonstration of love towards His creation. In the world in which we live, people are desperately searching with the hope of discovering some type of meaning for their incomplete, out of control and frustrated lives. God is the origin of our existence and in this, we as His creation find meaning for our lives, which results from the goal, purpose, or destiny He intends for us.

The greatest expression of love that we can demonstrate is to "'Love the Lord your God with all your heart and with all your soul and with all your strength and with all your mind'; and, 'Love your neighbor as yourself'" *(Lk. 10:27).*

We have been created in the image of love, which should remind us of God's love for each one of us and that we are worthy of His love. We must never forget "God loves you just the way you are, but he refuses to leave you that way. He wants you to be just like Jesus" (Lucado 1998:3). It should also remind us that each person must be responsible to live according to God's design for us. Each individual has been called to respond to God in love, walk in obedience to Him, and live out our true identity and purpose for our existence. Even though we may proclaim that humankind is created in the image of God, Jesus Christ alone is created fully in the divine image (2 Cor. 4:4; Col. 1:15). We as believers are in a process of "being transformed into his likeness with ever-increasing glory" (2 Cor. 3:18). This process of "being transformed" begins with faith in Jesus Christ and continues until we are brought into full conformity of God's divine purpose for us. Then we will truly be in the image of God.

The Community of Love and the Kingdom of God

Throughout the Old Testament we can see God establishing a community, a remnant with His people. From the beginning, Adam and Eve were placed in the Garden of Eden to enjoy communion with God. However, they chose to disobey God, which resulted in this communion being broken by choosing not to live under the gracious love and care of their Creator. In the Pentateuch, we see the call of Abraham, the covenant of grace being established between God and the patriarchs, the deliverance from bondage in Egypt, the giving of the Ten Commandments on Mount Sinai, and the wanderings in the wilderness, and finally the fulfillment of the Exodus, taking hold of the promise land.

True life is the result of giving up one's life and living in community with Jesus and with others. Therefore, we find our true identity as we participate with other members in the community of love.

In the historical books, we see God and His dealings with Israel and their judges and kings such as Saul, David, and Solomon, which was meaningless since they broke the Sinaitic Covenant and their apostasy with God. The result of this was that they experienced division and civil war and the Northern Kingdom of Israel was eradicated and the Southern Kingdom of Judah was forced into exile at Babylon. Even though God allowed the restoration of a portion of their civil and religious life, the Davidic rule was not restored.   Arthur F. Glasser distinguishes between the kingdom and the church,

> The Basileia creates a community, and uses a community as an instrument. Those who enter the Basileia are in the Ecclesia; the Ecclesia lives beneath the kingly rule of God, acknowledges it, proclaims it, and looks for its final manifestation, but the Ecclesia is not itself the Basileia. Since the church is gathered under God's rule, death will have no power over it (1989:205).

George Eldon Ladd brings the Kingdom of God down to earth and describes it as being personally involved through the community of Christ, His body. "The Kingdom is not primarily concerned with individual salvation or with the future but with the social problems of the present" (1959:16).

The Community of Love and Its Development

This is a process in which new social borders are defined and its external boundaries are distinguished by gates, fences or possibly by feelings of distinct characteristics. On the other hand, there are also internal boundaries, which distinguish those inside from those in the outside world (Keith 1982:4). The development of community within Scripture mirrors the changing religious, social, and political environment in which faith and life are in continuous transition.

Biblical community focuses on the worship of God, sharing with one another, experiencing salvation and a call to be witnesses of His salvation to the nations. Throughout Scripture, the history of Israel, the church, and community life was developed to correct problems with people of extreme faith. This biblical idea of community is balanced by two persuasive arguments:

> First, that a good God that finds forsaken persons who are alienated from all that makes for hope and well-being, and calls them into a covenant people reconciled to all that makes for peace and freedom;

and second, that this redeemed people then responds to God by embodying their experience of God's salvation in their relations with each other (Freedman 1992, 1:1103).

The Community of Love and Its Characteristics

Some of these characteristics include: interest, beliefs, occupation, activities, experiences, politics, and concerns. These characteristics are descriptive of the life within the Israelite community. First of all, community life involved the extended family which also had its place within the larger community or tribe. Second, community was based on the patriarchal structure, where the woman's role was defined by the male and his property rights. Third, the autonomy of each tribe was preserved by their recognition of the sovereignty of Yahweh. Fourth, their growth, and survival was attributed to their confession to God and deliverance from Egypt and the right of every family's use of designated land. Fifth, the most serious structural weakness was centrifugal tendencies, which continued through the autonomism of each tribe. This was a hindrance to the overall unity necessary to defend against hostile neighbors (Freedman 1992, 1:1104).

The Community of Love and Some Examples

Community carries the idea of one person engaged in communion with another. Some examples of this are: Enoch is described as a man who "walked with God" (Gen. 5:22, 24). Noah also "walked with God" (Gen. 6:9). Abraham is known as the "friend of God" (Jas. 2:23). Moses is known to have had the deepest communion with God during his forty-day encounter with God on Mount Sinai (Ex. 24). David wrote psalms that expressed his communion with God, however, some of them did not express intimate communion. Other examples of communion with God would include: Hagar (Gen. 16:8-12); Isaac (Gen. 26:2, 24; 28:12-15); Joshua (Jos. 1:1-9; 6:2-5); Gideon (Jud. 6:11-24); Solomon (1 Kgs. 3:5-14; 2 Ch. 1:7-12).

The Community of Love and Its Dangers

There are two primary dangers that hinder the community life. The first danger is individualism because it emphasizes personal privilege and self-importance and climaxes in abandoning the common structure that holds community life together. It insists on getting one's own way, and refusing to share one's belonging's with others or receive discipline from Christian brothers and sisters. It "turns the rightful and needed sense of individual responsibility before God, and the need for a personal experience of Christ and the Holy Spirit, into a corrupted spirit of self-exaltation" (Smith 1996:346). C. Norman Kraus continues this thought,

> In Old Testament society the worst fate individuals could suffer was to be cut off from their inheritance among God's people. By contrast, the greatest blessing was to be completely joined to and identified with God's people in the festival of worship. Individualism could only be viewed as alienation. Personal fulfillment came through allying oneself with the life and purposes of the group (1993:37).

The second danger is institutionalism because it establishes a type of church government where only a select few can minister, and all others are excluded from participation in the life of the community. This culminates in the stagnation of the church because its focus is not to deepen one's relationship with the Lord or to take care of the members of the community and their ministry within the body of believers. The church's community life ceases to function as intended and denies the very nature and existence of the church.

The Community of Love in the New Testament [13]

In the New Testament, the community of love is now in full force since the coming of the Holy Spirit, which had been prophesied in Joel 2:28-32, is now fulfilled on the Day of Pentecost. The fulfillment of the coming of the Holy Spirit has brought unity to the founding of the church.

New Testament Definition

The word most commonly used in the New Testament for community is πλῆθος *(pléthos)*, which refers to a great number or multitude, and is used seven times in Luke and seventeen times in Acts. It is used for measuring in number and then in size which denotes a number, amount or duration. In the LXX it means "plurality, totality, quantity." Some examples are "much, great, powerful" as in God's love is abundant as in Psalms 106:45 and His righteousness as in Isaiah 63:7 (Bromiley 1985:866).

In the Books of Luke and Acts, *pléthos* signifies a "crowd" with a variety of meanings. It is sometimes distinguished from that of a smaller group (Lk. 1:10; Acts 6:2, 5), and denotes the total number of a group (Acts 4:32; 14:4; 15:12). Sometimes πολύ *(polý)* is added to strengthen *pléthos* and indicates the greatness of the multitude. In Luke 12:1, the phrase "a crowd of many thousands" is translated as an innumerable multitude of people. Other references include ἐκκλησία *(ekklēsía)* (Acts 7:38; 19:32, 39, 41; Heb. 2:12, 23) and describes an assembly, a religious congregation, and συναγωγή *(synagōgḗ)* (Acts 13:43; Jas. 2:2) describes a synagogue, a bringing together (Vine 1952:764).

---

[13] For a discussion on Community Life in the Old Testament see Appendix A.

The Community of Love in Matthew 18

Jesus turns from the external situations that focused on Peter, the church, and the disciples to the internal situations of community life. Jesus desires that the disciples who live within a well-ordered society should not be preoccupied with one's position within this community, but with the greatness of God. Jesus is teaching that the essence of greatness lay in performing acts of service for others, without regard to age especially that of a child.

Jesus taught that children were dependent and trusted others until that trust was broken. Children are friendly and unconscious of one's position and race until adult prejudices spoil the friendship. The child is candid, lives in constant amazement, and finds life exciting until they are overwhelmed with adult pressures of life. For Matthew, to "become like little children" (18:3) one humbles himself, which is the guarantee of greatness in the kingdom (Buttrick 1951, 7:468). "The sense is not humbles himself as this little child humbles himself, but humbles himself until he is like this little child" (Bruce 1986:1139).

Next, Jesus discusses various sayings that concern the obligations of those who are a part of the life of the Christian community. Jesus shifts His focus from literal children to those who are new Christians in the community and causing them to sin, has drastic consequences. The phrase "'drowned in the depths of the sea,' was a common practice in Greek and Roman society, and rare among the Jews. Most millstones were hand tools for domestic use; here it is the heavy stone pulled around by a donkey" (Gaebelein 1984, 8:398). He acknowledges that situations will arise in life, which may cause someone of weak faith to stumble, and also personal temptations and if they have no self-control they will also be held accountable to God. The phrase "fire of hell" (Mt. 18:9) referred to the Valley of Hinnon (Gehenna) which was the place of refuse for the city of Jerusalem.

Jesus continues with the Parable of the Lost Sheep (Mt. 18:10-14) which also concerns "these little ones." Matthew's concern is the importance of the Messiah's community not bringing any harm to its members, and sharing His concern for the eternal welfare of "these little ones," the weak in faith, and the new converts. His concern is the leaders active role in the maturing of the believer's within the community. The main point in this parable is that God's love for each individual is not at the expense of other members, but that the community as a whole would not lose even one of its members.

The remainder of this chapter speaks about various methods of resolving disputes within the community. Jesus is teaching the disciples that if your brother sins against you go to him, not by judging him, but by convicting him of his fault in humility so that he may be redeemed. This thought is based upon Leviticus 19:17 which states "Do not hate your brother in your heart. Rebuke your neighbor frankly so you will not share in his guilt." If this does not bring results, Deuteronomy 19:15 is to be applied where one or two witnesses are involved. Jesus equated His messianic community with ancient Israel.

Finally, if he still does not respond, he must be excommunicated from the community. Each member of the community is to abide by the corporate judgment and the individual responsibility each believer has towards other members. This belief of binding and loosing is a heavenly sanction between the will of God and the functioning of the authorities within the church. Charles M. Laymon states it well, "the moral decisions of the community are to be equated with the moral judgments of God" (1971:632).

In rabbinic literature, the consensus was that a brother was to be forgiven three times and on the fourth, was not forgiven (Gaebelein 1984, 8:405). However, Peter thinking that he is more compassionate than others offers "up to seven times" (Mt. 18:21). In the pre-Israelite period, vengeance toward another had no limits and Jesus is saying that within the community of

God, mercy can have no limits and grace must be also displayed toward another without limits.

Jesus now gives an example of the role of forgiveness within the community. This parable is about a king who has forgiven the debts of his subjects more than they can ever forgive one another. Therefore, a person who fails to forgive the debt of another is to be excluded from the community since its pattern is that of forgiveness. Jesus is illustrating that the worst prison is an unforgiving heart and if we refuse to forgive others, then we are placing ourselves in an emotional prison to be tormented by our own actions.

Jesus warns us that unless we have a humble and repentant heart God cannot forgive us and that we reveal the true condition of our heart by the way we treat our brothers and sisters within the community.

Today, many Christians have received forgiveness but have not really experienced forgiveness in their hearts, which makes it difficult to share forgiveness with those who have offended them. We live in a society where we demand justice, continually seek self-satisfaction, which places us in an emotional prison. However, if we live according to forgiving others, sharing with others what God has shared with us, we will enjoy "righteousness, peace and joy in the Holy Spirit" (Rom. 14:17).

Jesus warns us that unless we have a humble and repentant heart God cannot forgive us and that we reveal the true condition of our heart by the way we treat our brothers and sisters within the community. Jesus is also stating that when our hearts are full of pride and revenge there can be no true forgiveness. Our response towards others must always be that of a gentle, humble, loving, and forgiving heart. This is something that through the rejection that I faced as a young boy from the age of three years old until I was thirteen to love, accept, and forgive others even though they were cruel to me.

The Community of Love in Luke 4:18-19

"The Spirit of the Lord is on me, because he has anointed me to preach good news to the poor. He has sent me to proclaim freedom for the prisoners and recovery of sight for the blind, to release the oppressed, to proclaim the year of the Lord's favor" (Lk. 4:18-19).

The church is to be a hospital for sinners, a place where the sinner, the hurting, the hopeless, the discouraged, the depressed, the frustrated, and the confused can find love, acceptance, forgiveness, guidance, and encouragement. The church exists to benefit the residents of its community by providing for their spiritual, physical, emotional, financial, intellectual, psychological, and social needs, which Jesus responded to spontaneously and never turned down a direct request for help. This healing involves the whole person! Jesus was sent as a prophet to preach, as a priest to heal, and as a king to proclaim liberty to the captives.

Jesus, in verse 18, focused first of all on proclaiming the gospel to the poor which applies to the poor in general, because it is the poor who sense their need and respond honestly to the message of Jesus. Their material deprivation often translates into spiritual sensitivity and humility, who respond appropriately to God's message of hope.

The adjective πτωχός (ptōchós) denotes complete destitution that forces the poor to seek the help of others by begging. Also, there was no system of state poor relief, and although food was distributed, it was only given to citizens, and not specifically for the poor. There was also no moral or religious glorifying of poverty, on the contrary, in social conflicts, the poor could not even invoke the help of the gods (Kittel and Friedrich 1964, 6:886). The Community Rule (Qumran) says:

No one who is afflicted with any human impurity may come into the assembly of God. Anyone who is afflicted in his flesh, maimed in hand or foot, lame or blind, or deaf and dumb or with a visible mark

on his flesh . . . may not enter to take their place in the midst of the
community (1 Qsa. 2:3-9). Jesus on the other hand, said "But when
you give a banquet, invite the poor, the crippled, the lame, the blind,
and you will be blessed. Although they cannot repay you, you will
be repaid at the resurrection of the righteous" (Luke 14:13-14). For
Him, it was the outcasts and the despised who were singled out to
be invited to the messianic banquet and to be included in his
community (Giles 1995:34).

In the Greco-Roman world, wealthy people usually invited
those of lower social status to a banquet so that they would
receive honor for helping those less fortunate. Jesus was
teaching the Pharisees that if they sought to receive blessings
from being hospitable they already received their reward. True
blessing was the result of inviting people who could not repay
would be divinely rewarded.

God rewards hospitality that comes from true righteousness
and these Pharisees desired personal benefit showed no sign of
true righteousness. Jesus taught that giving should never be
used to create clients, which cut at the heart of the issue
(Pentecost 1981:330). Jesus also taught that giving is only
giving when you give that which you cannot afford to give.
True giving does not expect something in return. It is giving
from the depths of one's heart.

No one can have a flame of indignation against the cruel callousness
of piled up wealth or devote himself with his whole-souled power to
the bringing in of a social order of more equal opportunity unless he
first has compassion for the poor. None of us can take our everyday
business or profession and lift it up out of the arid dust of mean
detail into something greatly inspired and inspiring unless the fire of
human emotion is burning within our hearts (Buttrick 1952, 8:90).

When we remember Jesus, do we find it more difficult to be
cruel, selfish, or pitiless? To remember Jesus is to have
something in us so drawn to Him that we are more eager to be
generous, understanding, compassionate, and kind toward
others.

Even though Luke omits "bind up the brokenhearted" from Isaiah 61:1, this holds a deep relevance to the actual spirit of Jesus' ministry. The word "brokenhearted" in the Greek, συντετριμμενους την καρδιαν, literally means "to crush completely, shattered; used for kindling that is heated and catches fire by friction; to grind, to rub" (Kittel and Friedrich 1964, 7:919). It was a sign of weakness in the Greek world when something breaks or is crushed and twisted and finally perishes altogether. The promise of binding the brokenhearted is for men and women who are broken in heart, inwardly. They are characterized as the humble, but not the maltreated; they are smitten by the knowledge of their sin and their guilt before God (Kittel and Friedrich 1964, 7:919).

Jesus was sent to heal the brokenhearted, to comfort and cure afflicted consciences, to give peace to those that were troubled and humbled for sins, and under a dread of God's wrath against them. He brought rest to those who were weary and heavy-laden, under the burden of guilt and corruption. Jesus touched life not only through joy and power, like the pagan ideas of gods that came down to earth had sometimes assumed. He brought the consciousness of the presence of God not only on the heights, but in the valleys also, not only in the lights, but in the shadows, not only in those moments when life soars up on wings, but in those other moments when it walks with lame and weary feet upon a heavy road (Buttrick 1952, 8:91).

Jesus next proclaims freedom to the "poor" who were "captives." In the Old Testament, reference to captives meant the exiled, but often it had spiritual overtones, especially since the Old Testament viewed the exile as the result of sin (Dt. 28-32; Ps. 79:11; 126:1; Isa. 42:7). The image here is of release from captivity; but in Luke 4, the picture includes release from sin and spiritual captivity. Since the judgment of captivity is tied to sin, Jesus' call to the poor is to come to God and accept His forgiveness, which results in their freedom.

The adjective αἰχμαλώτος *(aichmálotos)*, refers to a miserable person who stands in special need of God's help, having been swallowed up by a terrible enemy. The thought of war is carried over into the inner moral and religious struggle of man and for man. The Jews and Gentiles of this time had become prisoners of the world by Satan through the false teachings of the Gnostics and were being lead astray by introducing them to his own wisdom (Kittel and Friedrich 1964, 1:195).

Jesus continues with the recovery of sight to the blind. In the Greek τυφλός ἀνάβλεψιν refers not only to inability to see, but also to an inability to be seen, invisible, unclear, hidden, concealed. It also meant to inflate with conceit, to be high-minded, be lifted up with pride, and was used both physically and metaphorically. One cause of the widespread blindness in the southern Mediterranean countries was heredity, which might produce blindness at birth or later in life (Kittel and Friedrich 1964, 8:270).

Another cause was the common barbaric custom of blinding, practiced, or threatened by men as well as gods, whether in passion out of jealousy or revenge, or in war retribution, or for political motives. In

The church is only the church when it exists for others.

general it was regarded as impossible to cure blindness, but only the supernatural powers of a god-like man or a god, not the skill of the physician, could restore sight to the blind (Kittel and Friedrich 1964, 8:270). The phrase "to release the oppressed" τεθραυσμένους ἐν ἀφέσει, was probably taken from Isaiah 58:6, and means the same as "to heal the brokenhearted." While a prophet could proclaim the message of freedom for the oppressed, only Jesus could bring it to fulfillment.

Jesus, in verse 19 states "to proclaim the year of the Lord's favor." He came to let the world know that the God whom they had offended was willing to be reconciled to them, and to accept them upon new terms. This alludes to the year of release, or jubilee, which was an acceptable year to servants, who were freed from all debts. Jesus came to sound the trumpet of jubilee, and blessed were they that heard the joyful sound (Ps. 89:15). It was the acceptable time, the day of salvation.

The church exists to benefit the residents of its community by providing for their spiritual, physical, financial, emotional, psychological, and social needs. "The church is only the church when it exists for others. The church's task in the secular city is to be the *diakonos* of the city, the servant who bends himself to struggle for its wholeness and health" (Giles 1995:12). This is the essence of community life, reaching the lost, the hurting, the destitute, the brokenhearted, those with physical sicknesses, the lonely, the depressed, and the oppressed.

As the church reaches out to their communities, changed lives become the greatest advertisement of the healing power of God. People are searching for freedom from fear, guilt, worry, resentment, loneliness, and as the church reaches out with the healing hands of Jesus, changed lives become changed communities. D. L. Moody once said: "the Bible was not given to increase our knowledge, but to change our

> *This is the essence of community life, reaching the lost, the hurting, the destitute, the brokenhearted, those with physical sicknesses, the lonely, the depressed, and the oppressed.*

lives" (Warren 1995:220). This is the heart of the gospel! Each time the church meets someone's need, a good testimony invades the interpersonal network of that community.

This narrative is a very important part of my life since it involves the central aspects of the life of the community in which we all belong. We are the church and our responsibility is the welfare of the whole since "the body is a unit, though it is made up of many parts; and though all its parts are many, they form one body. So it is with Christ" (1 Cor. 12:12). The gifts mentioned in the preceding verses are a remembrance that they were given to unite each member and their gifting(s) to the one body, and not used to boast about individual success, which only builds walls between its members.

The Community of Love in Acts 4:32-35

"All the believers were one in heart and mind. No one claimed that any of his possessions was his own, but they shared everything they had. With great power the apostles continued to testify to the resurrection of the Lord Jesus, and much grace was upon them all. There were no needy persons among them. For from time to time those who owned lands or houses sold them, brought the money from the sales and put it at the apostles' feet, and it was distributed to anyone as he had need" (Acts 4:32-35).

The apostles who lived among non-believing coworkers were misunderstood and faced challenges to their values. The apostles selfless attitude does not reflect an ascetic ideal like some Greek and Jewish sects, rather they practiced placing value on the lives of people over material possessions. The apostles were not setting up an economic system here, but simply responded to each other with gracious, Christlike compassion. This type of behavior that continued until the late 2nd century was strenuously ridiculed by pagans until their values finally overwhelmed the church (Keener 1993:329-330).

Earlier Peter and John had faced the gathering together of the Sanhedrin (Acts 4:1-22) because they were boldly preaching and teaching about Jesus' resurrection. However, the apostles were gathering together a new Sanhedrin, a new community (Acts 4:31), which divine approval was made manifest with a second Pentecost, and resulted in an outward sign of an earthquake. This was a sign of inward inspiration by the Holy Spirit which gave them the ability or strength to speak boldly (Robertson 1930, 3:56).

In Acts 4:32, the apostles are commended for three things; first, they were "one in heart and mind" or in the Greek καρδία καὶ ψυχὴ μία. It "is not possible to make a sharp distinction between heart and soul, only that there was harmony in thought and affection . . . in the multitude of those who believed" (Robertson 1930, 3:60-61).

Second, "no one claimed that any of his possessions was his own." The Greek word ὑπαρχόντων, means "to be in existence" and "to belong to" signifying one's "possessions, renouncing one's right to private property" (Vine, Unger, and White 1985:477). The phrase ἅπαντα κοινά means "common, mutual, public or common property" (Brown 1986, 2:639). Third, "they shared everything they had." This style of fellowship with its implications of sharing possessions, is mostly absent in the Old Testament. The phrase "heart and soul" is frequent enough (Dt. 6:5; 10:12; 11:13), but connecting "one soul" with "shared everything they had" is so frequent in Hellenistic literature that there is no doubt to Luke's allusion to the Hellenistic *topos* concerning friendship that "friends hold all things together" (Johnson 1992:58).

In Acts 4:33, Luke seems to place the apostles in the middle of the community life, so that "authority" and "possessions" will reinforce each other. The "great power" of their proclamation is matched by their position in collecting and distributing the community possessions. The Greek word δυνάμει, means, "energy, power, might, great force, great ability, strength. It is sometimes used to describe the powers of the world to come to work upon the earth and divine power overcoming all resistance" (Hayford 1991:1563). The Greek word δυνάμει is used with μεγάλη to emphasize the greatness by which the apostles ministered of the Lord's resurrection. The word ἀπεδίδουν, means "primarily to give up, render, or give back . . . it acquired the specific meaning of giving something up which one must give up because of some kind of obligation; to pay one's vow" (Brown 1978, 3:134). The phrase (much grace) χάρις τε μεγάλη refers to

> That power which flows from God and accompanies the activity of the apostles giving success to their mission . . . charis designates not only the attitude of the gods but also that of men and can also

designate the physical causes of the benevolent gift, charm, attraction, and in the plural can mean amiable characteristics (Brown 1986, 2:115).

In Acts 2:47, the community enjoyed *charis* "with the whole people," but in 4:33, the people enjoyed the favor of God, which rests upon God's blessing rather than on human approval (Brown 1986, 2:86). In Acts 4:34,

> The Spirit-filled community exhibited a remarkable unanimity, which expressed itself even in the attitude to private property. Whereas the institution of a communal purse was explicitly regulated in writing at Qumran, the action taken by these early disciples of Jesus was intended to be voluntary. Members regarded their private estates as being at the community disposal (Bruce 1988:100).

The verbs used here denote customary behavior, and also serve to generalize what may have been exceptional acts of generosity (Johnson 1992:59). The richer members made provision for the poorer and for a period of time, no one had a need to complain of hunger or need of anything until funds ran out due to a famine (Acts 11:28) that the Jerusalem church became dependent on the generosity of fellow believers in other areas. The Greek word ἔφερον, means "to carry or bring from one place to another, then to be laden" (Bromiley 1974, 9:56). The word τιμὰς, means the "proper recognition which a man enjoys in the community because of his office, position, wealth, and then the position itself, the office with its dignity and privileges (Brown 1986, 2:48).

The witness of the Early Church was not the work of a chosen few, but a daily delight and ministry of the entire community.

In Acts 4:35, the phrase "laid them down at the apostles feet," refers "to being in a state of submission or obedience." It denotes "the body language of self-disposition spelled out by possessions, specifically acknowledges the power and authority of another over the self and what one has" (Johnson 1992:87). The apostles were the community leaders who received the goods that were brought, however, since they devoted their time and energy to their public witness of Jesus' resurrection, they needed to delegate the distribution to others, possibly deacons.

Their brotherly love for one another made each person's possessions common among the poor and needy, they looked at each other, especially the poor, with gratefulness and gave everything they had so that others could be blessed. Each member was an effective witness for Jesus Christ, no matter what happened to them or where they traveled and because of this the church grew from 120 in the Upper Room to over 8,000 in just a short time. Here is a picture of these 8,000 Christians in love with each other because each was in love with the Lord Jesus Christ and filled with the Holy Spirit.

There is no specification of person's type of need. Anyone with any type of need could receive the funds to meet their needs. The apostles recognizing their position of stewardship, dared not receive the possessions of the believers as their own personal property, but acted instead as trustees over the repository of the church's wealth, distributing daily to the individual's need (Hayford 1991:1563). Even though Satan tried to shake the faith of the Early Church, nothing could shake what God had shaken, stirred up, and established within the hearts and souls of this community.

Acts 4:32-35 involved a God-given spiritual unity, not a man-made organizational uniformity. The Early Church was a living organism that was held together by life, which comes through the Holy Spirit. This church was not a religious institution that existed just to keep itself alive, rather, it was united in doctrinal beliefs, fellowship, giving, and worship. People were drawn to the believers because their physical, spiritual, emotional, and psychological needs were being met through the church. The witness of the Early Church was not the work of a chosen few, but a daily delight and ministry of the entire community.

The Catalyst of the Community

The catalyst of the community is without a doubt the Holy Spirit whose purpose is to transform the lives of those who welcome Him. At the coming of the Holy Spirit (Acts 2:1-13), the symbols of wind and fire are represented, which describe the Holy Spirit's transforming power. At Pentecost the mysterious "violent wind" which dried up the Red Sea (Ex. 14:21), and whipped in the faces of the Israelites as they crossed to Sinai now again filled the house where they were assembled in "one accord."

The first symbol is "a sound from heaven, as of a rushing mighty wind, and it filled the whole house where they were sitting" (Acts 2:2, NJKV), which symbolized to all present, the presence of the Holy Spirit among them in a more intimate, more personal, and more powerful way than they had ever experienced before. It was the fulfillment of Jesus' prophecy in John 14:17. The coming of the Holy Spirit brought new life, empowerment for ministry, and boldness to be witnesses. The wind is a symbol of the Holy Spirit known in Ezekiel's prophecy (Eze. 37:9-14), which breathed new life into dead bones. Also, Jesus in speaking with Nicodemus uses the symbol of the wind of the Holy Spirit. Jesus describes that entrance into the new community requires a spiritual birth and that the Holy Spirit breathes where He wills. Therefore, as people cannot understand His work in our lives, neither can they understand anything born of the Spirit, which perplexed Nicodemus.

The second symbol is that "they saw what seemed to be tongues of fire that separated and came to rest on each of them" (Acts 2:3). "Tongues" symbolize the proclamation of the gospel and "fire" symbolizes God's purifying presence, which burns away the undesirable elements of our life and sets our heart aflame to ignite the lives of others. On Mount Sinai, God confirmed the validity of the Old Testament law with fire from heaven (Ex. 19:16-18). At Pentecost, God confirmed the

validity of the Holy Spirit's ministry by sending fire. On Mount
Sinai, fire came down upon one place. However, at Pentecost,
fire came down on many believers, which symbolized that
God's presence is available to all who believe in Him.

According to Rabbinic tradition, it was on Pentecost that Moses
received God's Law on Mount Sinai; it was believed, moreover, that
Moses had understood the law in 70 languages. It has been
suggested that a possible Lucan motif was connected to this idea:
"Just as the law which united Israel to the old covenant was
available to people in 70 languages, so the Spirit of God united the
new community of God in a new covenant with the capacity of
communicating the good news in all languages" (Smith 1996:252).

The Head of the Community

"That power is like the working of his mighty strength, which he
exerted in Christ when he raised him from the dead and seated him
at his right hand in the heavenly realms, far above all rule and
authority, power and dominion, and every title that can be given, not
only in the present age but also in the one to come. And God placed
all things under his feet and appointed him to be head over
everything for the church, which is his body, the fullness of him
who fills everything in every way" (Eph. 1:20-23).

The apostle Paul is praying for the Ephesian believers that
the Lord would "give you the Spirit of wisdom and revelation,
so that you may know him better." He also prays that "the eyes
of your heart may be enlightened in order that you may know
the hope to which he has called you, the riches of his glorious
inheritance in the saints" (Eph. 1:17-18). Paul describes the
awesomeness of the omnipotence of God ever exhibited since
the foundation of the universe, which is the raising of Jesus
from the dead and adorning Him with all power, both in heaven
and on earth.

The church is called "his body," and "his fulness." The body we
know, consists of many members: and it is the whole aggregate of
members that constitutes the body: and the body, joined to the head,

forms the complete man. This is the precise idea in the text. Every believer is a member of Christ: the whole collective number of believers from his entire body: and, by their union with him, Christ himself is represented as complete. The body would not be complete, if any member was wanting; nor is the Head complete without the body: but the body united to the Head is "the fulness," the completion of Christ himself (Simeon 1956, 17:285).

Characteristics of Community Life

The community life of the Early Church consisted of various characteristics, which distinguished it from all other patterns within Jewish society. One of the primary characteristic of the Early Church was that these "God-fearing Jews" "were all with one accord in one place" (Acts 2:2[14]). The phrase "one accord" is very significant because it speaks of the unifying presence of the Holy Spirit in gathering people together "from every nation under heaven (Acts 2:5), which is used eleven times in the Book of Acts.

The first reference speaks of the disciples, women, Mary, and her brothers in the Upper Room who "continued with one accord in prayer and supplication" (Acts 1:14). Second, the unity of everyone "from every nation under heaven" were present on the Day of Pentecost (Acts 2:1). Third, was the daily, unified adherence to the customary forms of their Jewish heritage (Acts 2:46). They more than just fellowshipped with one another in their homes, they also found favor among the people. Fourth, was the church's response to the release of Peter and John from prison and the spontaneous outburst of praise, adoration, and thanksgiving (Acts 4:24). Fifth, the apostles defy the orders of the Sanhedrin warning to stop their ministry of "signs and wonders" and continued to meet together (Acts 5:12).

---

[14] Bible References in this section will be taken from the New King James Version of the Bible.

Sixth, speaks of the stoning of Stephen and how the Sanhedrin officials attacked Stephen and dragged him out of the city and executed by stoning (Acts 7:57). Seventh, "the multitudes with one accord heeded the things spoken by Philip, hearing and seeing the miracles which he did" (Acts 8:6). Eighth, the people of Tyre and Sidon united to ask Herod for peace because he had become enraged with them. Ninth, was the Jerusalem decree, which required abstaining from "things offered to idols, from blood, from things strangled, and from sexual immorality" were not to be viewed as necessary for salvation (Acts 15:29).

These four requirements were rituals aimed at making fellowship possible between Jewish and Gentile Christians (Acts 15:25). Tenth, the Jews in a united effort attacked Paul and brought him into court under Gallio, because he was persuading "men to worship God contrary to the law" (Acts 18:13). Finally, is the riot in Ephesus, where Demetrius and other craftsmen were loosing business because Paul's traveling companions, Gaius and Aristarchus had "persuaded and turned away many people, saying that they are not gods which are made with hands" (Acts 19:26). After they were seized, the people rushed together as one man into the theater (Acts 19:29).

Another primary characteristic of the church is that it exists to bring glory to God. Throughout Scripture, the foundational purpose of all creation is to bring glory to God (Ps. 19:1). God created humankind as a special creation and the recipients of special concern and privileges. Therefore, we are to offer praise and worship to Him (Gen. 1:28; Ps. 147:1). Our ultimate motivation in planning, our goals, and our actions must be centered solely on our desire to bring glory to God. Everything we say and do must be done so that God will be glorified through us.

> "And whatever you do, whether in word or deed, do it all in the name of the Lord Jesus, giving thanks to God the Father through him" (Col. 3:17).

Chapter 3

Foundations For
Community Life

The purpose of this chapter is to describe the primary foundation to the life and ministry of the Early Church which included the coming of the Holy Spirit on the Day of Pentecost, prayer, worship, membership, water baptism, and the Lord's Supper. This chapter presents the fundamental concepts which governed the life and ministry of the Early Church. They viewed prayer as the life-giving force and without it there is nothing to sustain the believer. Everything they did was founded upon a life of prayer.

> "And being assembled together with them, He commanded them not
> to depart from Jerusalem, but to wait for the Promise of the Father,
> 'which,' He said, 'you have heard from Me'" (Acts 1:4, NJKV).

From the beginning, God has desired a universal covenant community under His rule. However, in the story of Babel, humankind through pride and pretension thought that they could construct their own community independent of God in order to save themselves. This was accomplished under the leadership of Nimrod who established his reign in "Babel (Babylon), Erech, Akkad, Calneh, in Shinar" (Gen. 10:10; 11:1-9), which resulted in God's judgment being poured out upon them and the disintegration of this community. "That is why it was called Babel—because there the Lord confused the language of the whole world. From there the Lord scattered them over the face of the whole earth" (Gen. 11:9). The Tower of Babel also saw the multiplication of cultures. The scattering of the nations provides the setting for God's covenant promise, "I will make you into a great nation and I will bless you; I will make your name great, and you will be a blessing" (Gen. 12:2). It would be through Abraham that all the families of the earth would be blessed with salvation.

In partial fulfillment of this promise, the Lord saved Israel by delivering them from slavery in Egypt, where they had lost their identity as Yahweh's people. The Lord now forms them into a community and through Moses reestablishes the covenant with them that He had made with Abraham and Sarah. Jesus, who "came to seek and to save what was lost" (Lk. 19:10), also brought this promise to fulfillment when He called the Jews into a community way of life. When the Jews refused the messianic claims of Jesus, He formed a new community of disciples, which culminated in the coming of "the promise of the Father" at Pentecost. When the Jewish audience came to believe that Jesus really was the Messiah, on the Day of Pentecost, they gathered together as a community in expectation of His return.

> Just as Israel received their new identity as the people of God at Sinai through the gift of the Torah (Law), so the new people is constituted through the gift of the Spirit. And just as great signs accompanied Israel's deliverance and formation into a covenant nation, so "signs and wonders done through the apostles" accompanied the birth of the new community of the Spirit (Kraus 1993:20).

The Promise of the Father

It has been said that there are approximately 8,000 promises throughout Scripture, however, "the promise of the Father" (Acts 1:4, NKJV) uniquely relates to the coming of the Holy Spirit on the Day of Pentecost. Various passages speak of "the promise of the Father." First, is Jesus appearance to His disciples just before His ascension, "Behold, I send the Promise of My Father upon you; but tarry in the city of Jerusalem until you are endued with power from on high" (Lk. 24:49, NKJV). This empowerment of the Holy Spirit will affect their role as witnesses. The second is at the time of Jesus' ascension, "And being assembled together with them, He commanded them not to depart from Jerusalem, but to wait for the Promise of the Father, 'which,' He said, 'you have heard from Me;'" (Acts 1:4, NJKV).

Third, Peter's sermon on the Day of Pentecost refers to the coming of the Spirit that had been experienced (Acts 2:1-4) by himself and many others, "Therefore being exalted to the right hand of God, and having received from the Father the promise of the Holy Spirit, He poured out this which you now see and hear" (Acts 2:33, NJKV). Finally, also on the Day of Pentecost, Peter declared that the gift of the Holy Spirit was synonymous with "the promise of the Father" was extended not only to Peter's audience, but also to their children, and those "who are far off" (Ervin 1987:28).

> "Then Peter said to them, 'Repent, and let every one of you be baptized in the name of Jesus Christ for the remission of sins; and you shall receive the gift of the Holy Spirit. For the promise is to you and to your children, and to all who are afar off, as many as the Lord our God will call'" (Acts 2:38-39, NJKV).

The coming of the Holy Spirit was not a one-time occurrence; it was not limited to the disciples, but was to be a continual experience in the lives "as many as the Lord our God will call."

> Pentecost was nonrepeatable. But it was not merely a passing occasion of prophetic fulfillment. Nor do the effects of this event end in the upper room and with the disciples who were gathered there. On the contrary, the coming of the Spirit marked the inauguration of the age of fulfillment (1 Peter 1:10-12). And the reality of Pentecost embraces all believers. All now enjoy the presence of the Spirit, who forms us into one fellowship. Hence, Paul declared, "For we were all baptized by one Spirit into one body . . . and we were all given the one Spirit to drink" (1 Cor. 12:13). Insofar as we are joined to the community of Christ, we all participate in the Pentecost experience, which is the reception of the endowment and the empowerment of the Spirit. In fact, Paul declared that if we do not "have" the Spirit we do not even belong to Christ (Rom. 8:9). Pentecost, then, was an event of the Church (Grenz 1994:482).

Howard M. Ervin also states

> The purpose of Pentecost is unmistakenly world evangelism, and
> the progress of the gospel is determined by the outline of Acts 1:8. .
> . and the empowerment with the Spirit has not yet been fulfilled.
> Jesus' commission is still in effect, and so too is the charismatic
> enduement with power given to realize this purpose (1987:38).

There are other accounts referring to "the promise of the
Father," however, they are not directly pointed to the same
event of Pentecost. The closest reference is the Caesarean
account, which speaks of a centurion named Cornelius and his
Italian regiment, had received "the gift of the Holy Spirit had
been poured out on the Gentiles also" (Acts 10:45, NJKV).
Also, Paul speaks of receiving "the promise of the Spirit
through faith" in Galatians 3:14, and in Ephesians 1:13 about
"the Holy Spirit of promise." Therefore, all of these references
point to the fact that "the promise of the Father" continues
throughout the ages.

The Exaltation of Jesus

> "But I tell you the truth: It is for your good that I am going away.
> Unless I go away, the Counselor will not come to you; but if I go, I
> will send him to you" (Jn. 16:7).

There is an illuminating sequence that occurs beginning
with John 14:16 and ending with John 16:7. First, the Father
will give the Holy Spirit at the request of Jesus (Jn. 14:16).
Second, the Father will send the Holy Spirit in Jesus' name (Jn.
14:26). Third, Jesus will sent the Holy Spirit from the Father
(Jn. 15:26). Finally, Jesus sends the Holy Spirit (Jn. 16:7).
Two important facts are presented here. The first is that it is
better for the disciples not to be dependent upon the physical
person of Jesus. However, more importantly, Jesus could not
send the Holy Spirit until He had ascended and took His rightful
place at the right hand of His Father (Eph. 1:18-23). The reason

for this was that the Holy Spirit could not be sent "because Jesus was not yet glorified" (Jn. 7:39).

Leon Morris states,

> So now the implication is that the cross is critical. Before that Jesus could not send the Spirit. Afterward he will send him (cf. 15:26). It is the divine concern to bring about a full salvation for people. That salvation can be based on nothing but Christ's atoning work. Only when that is accomplished can people receive the Spirit in all his fullness (1995:618).

Constituting Factors of the Early Church

As Luke begins his second book he serves to unify both the books of Luke and Acts, which stress factors that constitute the life of the Early Church. The first factor is a continuation from Luke 24:45-53, which is a prelude to the outpouring of the Holy Spirit and the expansion of the mission church (Acts 1:1-5). The second factor is the mandate to be witnesses (Acts 1:6-8). These verses contain the central theme of the Early Church, and sets the stage for the remainder of the Book of Acts, "But you will receive power when the Holy Spirit comes on you; and you will be my witnesses in Jerusalem, and in all Judea and Samaria, and to the ends of the earth" (Acts 1:8). The third factor is the ascension of our Lord and Savior Jesus Christ (Acts 1:9-11). The point that Luke makes here is more than the mandate to be witnesses, but on Jesus' ascension and taking His rightful place in heaven, the descension of the Holy Spirit, and His imminent return.

The fourth factor is the focus on the ministry of the apostles. Luke had spoken of the designation of the apostles (Lk. 6:13), and now he resumes by describing God's direction and restoration of the twelve apostles after Judas' defection. The final factor is the outpouring of the Holy Spirit on the Day of Pentecost (Acts 2:1-41). This advent of the Holy Spirit is the culmination of the previous four factors, which includes the baptism of the Holy Spirit and Peter's inaugural sermon, which unifies these events (Gaebelein 1981, 9:252-268).

Community Life and Structure

It is interesting that Jesus made only a little contribution to the structure and establishment of an orderly pattern of life and ministry in the Early Church. However, He left this work to the Holy Spirit who is the administrator of spiritual gifts. Before Jesus ascended, He instituted the basic elements such as the calling of the twelve disciples, the giving of the Great Commission, the institution of the Lord's Supper, water baptism, and gave the Sermon on the Mount.

The Early Church did not have an institutional or organizational structure, but was the community of God's people. In Scripture, church structure can be evaluated using the following criteria. First, it must be biblically valid. It must be in harmony with the nature and form of the gospel and the church. It should aid the church in becoming what it already is, and also fulfill its mission. Its structure must establish and promote community, train disciples, and be a vital witness to its community. Second, it must be culturally relevant. The church must be in harmony with the culture in which it exists. The church of one culture cannot be transplanted within another without creating some type of tension. The transplanting of a church in another culture must be culturally relevant without compromising the message of the gospel.

Third, it must be flexible. It must be capable of responding or conforming to changing or new situations. Since cultures are in a state of continual change, church structure must also change as the culture changes. Therefore, biblical validity takes priority over cultural relevancy and flexibility. Even though the church will never escape tension between itself and the culture in which it exists, it must always remain true to its foundation, Jesus Christ.

The Book of Acts presents the Early Church with an informal organizational structure. Therefore, a person's ecclesiology must be taken from the epistles and the gospels, rather than the Book of Acts. However, the Book of Acts is the best source of how the Early Church functioned and was structured. It describes how the needs of the community were recognized and provided for by the Early Church. These needs included prayer, worship, meeting together in house churches, the family, nurture, and the witness of the community.

The Pattern of the Synagogue

The term συναγωγὴ *(synagōgé)* refers to "bringing together or assembling (cf. a gathering of people, a collection of books or letters, the ingathering of harvest, the mustering of troops, the knitting of brows, the drawing in of a sail, and in logic the deduction or demonstration)" (Bromiley 1985:1108). It was the custom of the apostle Paul when he entered a city to first go into the synagogue and preach as long as he was allowed to do so (Acts 17:1).[15] Ferguson states, "the word synagogue referred to the assembly of people and came to be applied to the building where the assembly occurred and then to the related institutional life" (1993:539). The *Universal Jewish Encyclopedia* states that the synagogue has no exact date of origin.

> They were unknown in the pre-Exilic period. During the Babylonian Exile, people used to assemble at the house of a prophet, or other leader. The synagogue must have developed during the early centuries of the post-Exilic period. Ps. 74:8, which probably described the Syrian persecution (168-165 B.C.E.), bewails the burning of "all the meeting-places of God in the land," a statement which implies that synagogues were then found throughout Palestine. The oldest dated evidence comes from Egypt,

---

[15] "The Acts of the Apostles refers to synagogues in Jerusalem (6:9), Damascus (9:2), Cyprus (13:5), the Roman province of Galatia (13:14; 14:1), Macedonia and Greece (17:1, 10, 17; 18:4), and Ephesus in the province of Asia (19:8)" (Elwell 1988, 2:2008).

where the synagogue at Schedia was dedicated to King Ptolemy III (247-221) and Queen Bernice. Evidently the country had numerous synagogues by about 250 B.C.E. the Jews must have begun to establish them shortly after their settlement at the end of the 4th century. In the same way the synagogue has accompanied the Jews in their wanderings over the earth. To this day, wherever Jews settle in sufficient numbers, they erect a synagogue on their own initiative, without official compulsion (Landman 1943, 10:120).

The synagogue was considered the center of the community, religious, and social life of the Jews. It provided the setting for the teachings of Jesus, the apostles, the gathering place of the Christian converts, worship and organization of the Early Church. It also organized a system of administering the activities commanded in the law, and was used as a place of teaching the law and the prophets, a house of prayer, a house of meeting, and a house of judgment (Ferguson 1993:540). "Its central enduring purpose was the proclamation and exposition of the law. Every synagogue possessed a Torah scroll from which the law was proclaimed, and it was this proclamation that gave the synagogue its reason for being" (Cassidy 1978:107).

Kenneth S. Latourette states, "the synagogue has risen between the revival of Judaism after the fall of the Northern and Southern Kingdoms and the time of Jesus. Until its destruction a generation or so after the time of Jesus, the temple in Jerusalem was the main shrine of Judaism" (1975, 1:13). Paul used both the Judaic and synagogue pattern as the structure for his church planting and missionary endeavors.

The early church community borrowed its basic structure from the synagogue: "Let us recognize the structure so fondly called 'The New Testament Church' as basically a Christian synagogue." The new churches planted by Paul, in particular, were "essentially built along Jewish synagogue lines, embracing the community of the faithful in any given place." The really unique thing about these new communities was their ability through the reconciling work of Christ to break down "the dividing wall of hostility" between Jew and Gentile and bring both together in one open fellowship (Eph. 2:11-22). The common pattern of the church in the New Testament was a synagogue type of community which centered around large-group corporate worship and small-group fellowship and worship cells meeting primarily in homes (Synder 1977:151).

Prayer in the Early Church

"Now it came to pass, as He was praying in a certain place, when He ceased, *that* one of His disciples said to Him, 'Lord, teach us to pray, as John also taught his disciples.' So He said to them, 'When you pray, say: Our Father in heaven, Hallowed be Your name. Your kingdom come. Your will be done on earth as *it is* in heaven. Give us day by day our daily bread. And forgive us our sins, for we also forgive everyone who is indebted to us. And do not lead us into temptation, but deliver us from the evil one'" (Lk. 11:1-4, NKJV).

Jesus' model prayer contains three petitions concerning the holiness and the will of God, and three petitions concerning our personal needs that should be a priority in the Christians life.

Prayer Among the Jews

When we think of the Lord's Prayer, do we ever wonder about its origin. Jesus' implementation of the Lord's Prayer is faithful to Jewish formulas. Jesus used biblical and Jewish prayers to formulate the Lord's prayer, which is seen in Table 1.

Jesus brings new life into His body, through creating Christian prayer from the foundations of Jewish prayer. He created the Lord's Prayer so that it would involve both Jews and Gentiles in one faith in Himself. Jesus did not intend to change what they were used to reciting, He just made it better through expressing the plentitude of Yahweh concisely and clearly. Like the Law, Jesus did not come to abolish the prayer life of the Jews, He came to fulfill it, to give a deeper meaning to their devotion to God. "Do not think that I have come to abolish the Law or the Prophets; I have not come to abolish them but to fulfill them" (Mt. 5:17).

Table 1

The Jewish Roots of the Lord's Prayer
(Hamman 1971:105-108)

The Lord's Prayer	The Bible	Shemone Esre[16]	Kaddish[17]	The Rabbis
Our Father in Heaven.			May the heavenly Father receive the prayer of all the house of Israel.	
May your name be held holy.	I mean to display the holiness of my great name (Ez. 36, 23; cf. Ps. 111, 9).	You are holy and your name is wonderful (3).	May your great name be exalted and sanctified.	Our Father who art in heaven, may your name be praised through all the eternities (Seder Elij. SB. I, 410).
Your will be done on earth as in heaven	God is in heaven, you are on earth (Qo. 5, 1; I M. 3, 60).			Do your will in heaven, on high, and grant a calm courage to those who fear you on earth (R. Eliezer, SB. I, 419-420).

---

16 "'Hear, O Israel: the LORD our God is one Lord' (Deut. 6:4), later expanded by verses 5-9; 11:13-21; Numbers 15:37-41. Shema is the Hebrew word behind 'Hear.' Shemone Esreh means 'eighteen,' but in fact the number of benedictions has varied from time to time" (Gundry 1994:63).

17 "A word meaning 'Sanctification,' and the name of prayer written in Aramaic. It was originally recited after study and at the end of important portions of the daily liturgy in the synagogue, but for many centuries has also been used as a mourner's prayer" (Bridger 1976:259).

Give us this day our daily bread.	Give me neither poverty nor riches, grant me only my share of bread to eat (Pr. 30, 8; cf. Ex. 16, 4; Ps. 147, 9).	Bless Yahweh our God, this year (9).		May God be blessed every day for the bread he gives us (SB. 1, 421).
And forgive us our debts as we have forgiven those who are in debt to us.	Forgive your neighbor the hurt he does you, and when you pray, your sins will be forgiven (Si. 28, 2).	Forgive us, our Father, for we have sinned against you, wipe away our iniquities; remove them from your sight (6).		Our Father, our King, pardon and remit all our faults, remove and wipe away our sins from before your eyes (Avinu malkenu, SB. I, 421).
And do not put us to the test.				Do not lead us into the power of sin, nor into the power of error, nor into the power of temptation, nor into the power of betrayal. May I be ruled by the power of good, and not by the power of evil (SB. I, 422).
But save us from		See our need and		Save us from the impudent and

the evil one.		fight our combat, and deliver us for the sake of your name (7).		from impudence, from the evil man, from evil encounters, from the strength of evil, from evil companions, from evil neighbors, from Satan the corruptor, from your strict judgment, from a bad adversary at the tribunal (Berakhot, SB., I, 422).
(Doxology) For yours is the kingdom and the power and the glory forever. Amen.	Yours Yahweh, is the greatness, the power, splendor, length of days, glory Yours is the sovereignty Yahweh (1 Ch. 29, 11).			

The Lord's Prayer is divided into two parts: the first three supplications are a revelation of God in the Old Testament, while the last three are a revelation of the harmony with the newness of the gospel of Jesus Christ. The phrase "May your name be held holy" summarizes the first revelation that God made to Moses concerning His transcendence (Ex. 19:20-25). God chose a people who would be His witnesses to the nations of the earth. "Your kingdom come" expresses Yahweh's desire to make a nation of these scattered Hebrews and then gather them into His kingdom. "Your will be done" expresses the "Disaster, the exile, suffering, humiliation that prepared the way for the understanding necessary to read the Law from within, to find therein the Father's benevolent will, and to respond to it, by inward conversion, in an exchange of love" (Hamman 1971:109).

> "Forgive us our debts" *is not referring to an unbeliever because they have not been justified and freed from guilt through the atoning work of Jesus on the cross. It refers to the believer extending forgiveness to others not on the basis of their salvation, but on the basis of daily fellowship with our Father. Forgiving others reveals the reception of God's forgiveness.*

The phrase "give us today our daily bread" refers back to the Israelites in the wilderness, where they learned to trust God for manna daily. In the New Testament, it also refers to the people trusting God for sufficient food daily since workers were only hired on a daily basis (cf. Mt. 20:1-16). Jesus made sure that the people received daily both physical food and spiritual food. "Forgive us our debts" is not referring to an unbeliever because they have not been justified and freed from guilt through the atoning work of Jesus on the cross. It refers to the believer extending forgiveness to others not on the basis of their salvation, but the on basis of daily fellowship with our Father. Forgiving others reveals the reception of God's forgiveness.

The phrase "do not put us to the test" does not imply that God might tempt us to do evil (Jas. 1:1-15), however, it refers to God allowing His people to be tested as to their faithfulness. The Christian life implies daily confrontation with temptation and the tempter, and Jesus' victory is the foundation to our confidence in our prayer. "Save us from the evil one" is used metaphorically and refers to "being forcibly rescued from a dangerous situation while on a journey" (Hamman 1971:133).

Therefore, Jewish prayer was a continual earnest request for God to rescue His people from all troubles (Ps. 22:21; 54:7; 91:3; 142:7: 143:9). Most manuscripts do not include "For yours is the kingdom and the power and the glory forever. Amen."

In New Testament times, there were Jews who lived in every area of the Roman Empire. It was calculated that there were more Jews living in Egypt than there were in Jerusalem. Therefore, when Paul journeyed throughout Asia Minor, Macedonia, and the rest of the known world, he discovered that there were Jewish communities everywhere he traveled. In most places, the Jews had established synagogues and met regularly, and held prayer and worship services. The *Universal Jewish Encyclopedia* states that

> Prayer, as the ethical monotheism of Judaism conceives it, is the expression of child-like trust in God, of submission and resignation to the will of God, and, within certain movements of Judaism, the proper means of union with God. Jewish prayer is based upon the idea of the covenant between God and Israel, the hope in the future deliverance, the feeling of exaltation, and the doctrine of the kingdom of God; it is the intuitive and voluntary expression of that inner connection with God which remains indestructible despite all the vicissitudes of destiny which have befallen or may befall the Jewish people and the individual Jew (Landman 1942, 8:617).

The origin of prayer can be traced back to the Israel, where prayer occurred occasionally, which had its roots in the needs of the moment or a special cause. Public and private prayer began to develop only after the destruction of the first temple in 586 B.C. It was Jeremiah who developed the thought of a more personal relationship between man and God and Scripture, which indicates that individuals prayed to God from their homes (Ps. 42:9; 63:6-7; 119:62; 149:5). Sacrifice was accompanied by prayer, even though one was sometimes separated from the other. In the synagogue, prayer was attached to the reading of the Scripture.

Private prayer developed before public prayer; even after the later had become common, it remained in the public devotions in the form of silent prayer after the congregational prayers.

God is often addressed as Abinu Shebashamayim (Our Father, Who art in heaven), El Male Rahamim (God, rich in mercy), El Harahamim (God of mercy), Ab Harahamim (Father of mercy), Ribbono shel Olam (Lord of the world) (Landman 1943, 10:618).

There were several traditions that existed among the Jews. First, praying in the synagogue with the congregation was preferred over praying in one's home. Second, prayers were said in Hebrew. Third, prayers were said three times per day; morning, afternoon, and evening (Dan. 6:11). Fourth, when the *Amidah* was recited, the Jews stood with their legs together and their heads bowed. Fifth, prayer was a serious matter and complete concentration, without interruption or distraction was enforced. Sixth, prayer was always done facing Jerusalem or the Temple. Seventh, prayer was to be offered with pure motives. In Jewish tradition there was only three types of prayers; adoration, thanksgiving, and petition. The Book of Psalms was used as a book of prayers (Bridger 1976:390).

Finally, the beginning of the 2nd century B.C. saw the implementation of the phylactery, which was to be worn on the forehead and the left arm. These were visible during morning prayers, except on the Sabbath and at high festivals. They contained four passages from the Old Testament (Ex. 13:1-10, 13:11-16; Dt. 6:4-9; 11:13-21), written by hand on parchment. The Jew speaks of $t^e pill\hat{a}$ (lit. "prayer"), pl. $t^e pill\hat{i}n$. Their present form became standardized by the early years of the 2nd century A.D. and consists of two hollow cubes made of the skin of clean animals (Douglas 1962:938).

Prayer Among the Gentiles

The prayer life of the Gentiles was almost the same as the Pharisees. Their prayers were lengthy, long, and repetitious without any heart-felt communion with God. They believed that their gods would only hear them if they cried out, with importunate fervor, the same phrase many times. They would make passionate appeals to gods knowing that they would not receive any answer. The Word of God gives us glimpses of their devotion to prayer as they were educated and were observed by the people of Israel (Thirtle 1915:20).

Some examples of this type of prayer life can be seen by the worshippers of Baal, which Elijah confronted, "from morning till noon. 'O Baal, answer us!' they shouted. But there was no response; no one answered" (1 Kgs. 18:26). In the New Testament we have the example of Paul, on a missionary visit, as the Ephesians begin a riot because he was teaching "that man-made gods are no gods at all" (Acts 19:26). "But when they realized he was a Jew, they all shouted in unison for about two hours: 'Great is Artemis of the Ephesians!'" (Acts 19:34).

Jesus placed both the Jews and the Gentiles in the same category where He condemned their patterns of prayer. To the Jews, the Gentiles were hypocrites, because the gods that they served were false, and their worship was idolatrous flattery not ordained by God. Israel was influenced by the foolishness and impiety of the Gentiles, since they used "vain repetitions as the heathen do" (Mt. 6:7). Jesus condemns them for their use of "vain repetitions," however, what He wants to teach them concerns much praying. Jesus, in the Garden of Gethsemane, used repetition when he prayed three times "My Father, if it is possible, may this cup be taken from me. Yet not as I will, but as you will" (Mt. 26:39). Jesus "spent the night praying to God" (Lk. 6:12), which suggests that He also used repetition in His prayers. Therefore, it is not much praying that is his focus of condemnation, but of "vain repetition," which was thought to persuade a reluctant God to answer and was practiced throughout the East.

Jesus uses the acronym "ask" to describe how His disciples are to pray (Mt. 7:7-8). Jesus disciples will pray ("ask") with earnest sincerity ("seek"), and walk in an active, diligent pursuit of God's way ("knock"). The best gifts are available to

"everyone" (v. 8) who persistently asks, seeks and knocks
(Gaebelein 1984, 8:186). This persistence is also seen in the
parable of the persistent widow (Lk. 18:1-5).

Jesus confronted the Jews for leaving the ways of God and
following after the practices of the Gentiles. This confrontation
refers to the synagogue prayers, which were memorized and
passed down from generation to generation (Thirtle 1915:24).
This became the background that Jesus' public ministry needed
to confront and bring about a change in their prayer life.

Prayer Among the Christians

Jesus and the Early Church taught us the key to living
victoriously. Prayer is the life-sustaining responsibility of the
Christian life and a Christian who does not pray does not know
God and cannot therefore be called a Christian.

> Acts is an excellent link between the Gospels and the Epistles,
> because in Acts the apostolic church puts into effect our Lord's
> teaching on prayer. The church was born in the atmosphere of
> prayer (1:4). In answer to prayer the Spirit was poured out upon her
> (1:4; 2:4). Prayer continued to be the church's native air (2:42; 6:4,
> 6).
>   There remained in the church's thinking a close connection
> between prayer and the Spirit's presence and power (4:31). In times
> of crisis the church had recourse to prayer (4:23ff.; 12:5, 12).
> Throughout the Acts the church leaders emerge as men of prayer
> (9:40; 10:9; 16:25; 28:8) who urge the Christians to pray with them
> (20:28, 36; 21:5) (Douglas 1962:960).

Jesus gave us the greatest example of how to pray through
His life of prayer and devotion to His Father. The Lord's
Prayer (Mt. 6:9-13; Lk. 11:2-4) is also known as "The
Disciples' Prayer." There are no singular pronouns in this
prayer; they are all plurals (our, us, your). Prayer prepares us
for the proper use of the answer. If we know our need, and if
we voice it to God, trusting Him for His provision, then we will

make better use of the answer than if God forced it on us without our asking.

Literally, the Lord's Prayer reads "Lord, teach us to be praying," which expresses a continual action. Jesus was teaching His disciples to imitate Him in His habits of personal devotion (cf. Lk. 3:21; 6:12; 9:28). The disciples desired to be like Jesus, though being in the world, He was not of this world (Jn. 17:16). He demonstrated that to be in the presence of His Father was delightful, not a ritual that must be done regularly.

Almsgiving, prayer, and fasting (the "acts of righteousness") were the "three pillars" of Jewish piety (Mt. 6:1-18). The issue for Jesus is not whether one does them (each section begins, "When you . . ."), but how and why. Once we are secure in our relationship with the Father and His will, then we can bring our requests to Him. We can ask Him to provide our needs (not our greeds!) for today, to forgive us for what we have done yesterday, and lead us in the future. All of our needs may be included in these three requests: material and physical provision, moral and spiritual perfection, and divine protection and direction. If we pray this way, we can be sure of praying in God's will. Jesus taught His disciples to pray on various occasions such as:

Table 2

The Prayer Life of Jesus

At His Baptism	"When all the people were being baptized, Jesus was baptized too. And as he was praying, heaven was opened and the Holy Spirit descended on him in bodily form like a dove. And a voice came from heaven: 'You are my Son, whom I love; with you I am well pleased'" (Lk. 3:21-22).
Before Selecting His Apostles	"One of those days Jesus went out to a mountainside to pray, and spent the night praying to God. When morning came, he called his disciples to him and chose twelve of them, whom he also designated apostles" (Lk. 6:12-13).
At His Transfiguration	"About eight days after Jesus said this, he took Peter, John and James with him and went up onto a mountain to pray. As he was praying, the appearance of his face changed, and his clothes became as bright as a flash of lightning" (Lk. 9:28-29).
In the Garden of Gethsemane	"Then Jesus went with his disciples to a place called Gethsemane, and he said to them, 'Sit here while I go over there and pray'" (Mt. 26:36).
On the Cross	"Jesus said, 'Father, forgive them, for they do not know what they are doing.' And they divided up his clothes by casting lots. Jesus called out with a loud voice, 'Father, into your hands I commit my spirit.' When he had said this, he breathed his last" (Lk. 23:34, 46).
The Lord's Prayer	"One day Jesus was praying in a certain place. When he finished, one of his disciples said to him, 'Lord, teach us to pray, just as John taught his disciples.' He said to them, 'When you pray, say: Father, hallowed be your name, your kingdom come. Give us each day our daily bread. Forgive us our sins, for we also forgive everyone who sins against us. And lead us not into temptation'" (Lk. 11:1-4).
The High	"After Jesus said this, he looked toward heaven and prayed: 'Father, the time has come. Glorify your Son,

Priestly Prayer	that your Son may glorify you. Now this is eternal life: that they may know you, the only true God, and Jesus Christ, whom you have sent'" (Jn. 17:1, 3).

Jesus not only set an example of a life of prayer for His disciples to follow, He demonstrated various postures of prayer to show that there is no one formula of prayer that they needed to follow.

Table 3

Postures in the Prayer Life of Jesus

Kneeling	"He withdrew about a stone's throw beyond them, knelt down and prayed" (Lk. 22:41).
On His Face Before God	"Going a little farther, he fell with his face to the ground and prayed" (Mt. 26:39).
Standing	"And when you stand praying, if you hold anything against anyone, forgive him, so that your Father in heaven may forgive you your sins" (Mk. 11:25).

Jesus also stressed the fact that the life of a Christian involves daily devotion and communion with the Father and that without this the disciple lacks the strength and stamina to be bold and effective witnesses.

Table 4

Private Prayers of Jesus

Early Morning Prayer	"Very early in the morning, while it was still dark, Jesus got up, left the house and went off to a solitary place, where he prayed" (Mk. 1:35).
Evening Prayer	"After leaving them, he went up on a mountainside to pray" (Mk. 6:46).
Solitary Prayer	"Yet the news about him spread all the more, so that crowds of people came to hear him and to be healed of their sicknesses. But Jesus often withdrew to lonely places and prayed" (Lk. 5:15-16).
All Night Prayer	"One of those days Jesus went out to a mountainside to pray, and spent the night praying to God" (Lk. 6:12).
His Disciples With Him	"Once when Jesus was praying in private and his disciples were with him, he asked them, 'Who do the crowds say I am?'" (Lk. 9:18).
In Gethsemane	"He withdrew about a stone's throw beyond them, knelt down and prayed" (Lk. 22:41).

Jesus in teaching His disciples how to pray first needs to deliver them from their false ideas of prayer and teach them how to pray recognizing their deep need and God's abounding grace. The Lord's Prayer taught His disciples against practices that were vain and frequently impious. It was the custom in New Testament times for both Jews and Gentiles to make long prayers in formal devotions. The Rabbis believed

He that prays much is certain to be heard; Prolix prayer prolongeth life. Accordingly, worship became mechanical and lifeless, an insincere pretence, a ritualistic performance. The Pharisees found an occupation in such formalism, with the result that their lives were barren and unfruitful, and they laid themselves open to the charge of neglecting the weightier matters of "doing justly, loving mercy, and walking humbly with God" (Mic. 6:8) (Thirtle 1915:20).

However, Jesus taught a large crowd concerning the teachers of the law, "They devour widows' houses and for a show make lengthy prayers. Such men will be punished most severely" (Mk. 12:40). Frank E. Gaebelein states,

> Since the teachers of the law were not allowed to be paid for their services, they were dependent on the gifts of patrons for their livelihood. Such a system was vulnerable to abuses. Wealthy widows especially were preyed on by the greedy and unscrupulous among these men. Jesus particularly condemns the hypocrisy of their long prayers that were used as a mask for their greed (1984, 8:740).

Jesus, then uses the example of the widow's offering to contrast the greed of the teachers of the law with the generosity of the widow who out of her nothing gave everything.

Worship in the Early Church

Before the destruction of the temple in Jerusalem, the synagogue was the secondary place of worship in Palestine. Its origin was in the Diaspora communities of Egypt and Mesopotamia and was instituted in Palestine at the time the Hasmonean kingdom was established. Worship in the synagogue usually consisted of "the reciting of the shema" (confession of faith, Dt. 6:4-9), scripture readings from the Law and the Prophets, prayer, thanksgiving, and individual exhortations (Acts 13:15)" (Matthews 1995:259). Robert H. Gundry describes the typical synagogue service

> At first not very elaborate, the typical synagogue consisted of a rectangular room perhaps having a raised speaker's platform behind which rested a portable chest or shrine containing Old Testament scrolls. The congregation sat on stone benches running along two or three walls and on mats and possibly wooden chairs in the center

of the room. In front, facing the congregation, sat the ruler and elders of the synagogue. Singing was unaccompanied. To read from an Old Testament scroll, the speaker stood. To preach, he sat down. For prayer everyone stood. The typical synagogue service consisted of the following:

- Antiphonal recitations of the Shema[18] (Deut. 6:4ff., the "golden text" of Judaism) and the Shemone Esreh (a series of praises to God).
- Prayer
- Singing of psalms
- Readings from the Hebrew Old Testament law and prophets interspersed with a Targum, that is, a loose oral translation into Aramaic (or Greek), which many Jews understood better than Hebrew.
- A sermon (if someone competent at preaching was present)
- A blessing or benediction (1994:62).

The pattern of congregational worship was based on Acts 2:42, "they devoted themselves to the apostles' teaching and to the fellowship, to the breaking of bread and to prayer." Each member's talents were used to bring edification to the whole community (Rom. 12:3-8). In Paul's letter to Titus, he describes the qualities required to be an elder or leader in the church, however, "all of the adult members were to serve diligently as good examples to each other and the outside community as well" (Matthews 1995:261).

The Early Church established patterns of worship, which contrasted that of the synagogue worship. J. I. Packer, Merrill C. Tenney, and William White Jr. state,

---

[18] "One of the oldest and most important Hebrew prayers. Deriving its name from its first word, the *Shema* is held to be in a sense Israel's affirmation of faith: "Hear, O Israel, the Lord our God, the Lord is One." When the *Shema* is recited in the morning and evening services, it is accompanied by the reading of three other selections from the Pentateuch. Before retiring, only the first paragraph *(Veahavta)* is read. The reform practice is to be read only the one paragraph even at services" (Bridger 1976:445). "The Jewish confession of faith made up of Deut. 6:4-9 and 11:13-21 and Num. 15:37-41" (Mish 1993:1080).

We have no clear picture of early Christian worship until A.D. 150, when Justin Martyr described typical worship services in his writings. We do know that the early Christians held their services on Sunday, the first day of the week. They called this "the Lord's Day" because it was the day that Christ rose from the dead (1995:544).

They gathered in the Jerusalem temple, in synagogues, or in individual homes (Acts 2:46; 13:14-16; 20:7-8). Some scholars believe that the early Christians rented school buildings or other facilities to conduct their worship services and/or the teaching of doctrines. This was the case in Ephesus when Paul was "arguing persuasively about the kingdom of God" (Acts 19:8-10). Paul was teaching those who had received him favorably (cf. 18:19-21), however, opposition arose and Paul continued his teachings for two years in "the lecture hall of Tyrannus."[19]

There is no evidence that these early Christians built facilities to conduct their worship services until after the end of the 1st century. These Christians when encountered with persecution gathered in secret places like the catacombs of Rome. Most scholars agree that the early Christians worshipped late Sunday afternoon and later added an early Sunday morning service, which centered on the Lord's Supper. The hours of these services were chosen, first for secrecy, and second, because many people could not attend due to their work schedule. The order of these services was a time for praise, prayer, and preaching. Peter's sermon on the Day of Pentecost (Acts 2:14-42) probably followed the pattern that was used in the synagogue. They all shared hymns, testimonies and exhorted one another. "When you come together, everyone has

---

[19] "Codex Bezae (the important 'Western' text of Acts) adds that Paul taught from the fifth to the tenth hour (11:00 A.M. to 4:00 P.M.), a time not usually utilized by teachers of morality of this era for systematic instruction. It is not clear whether the hall of Tyrannus was a recognized center for moral instruction by philosophers or some sort of local trade union or guild center. It is highly unlikely that Paul's activity in the hall was systematic enough to be called a 'school' in any recognizable sense" (Achtemeier 1985:1101).

a hymn, or a word of instruction, a revelation, a tongue or an interpretation. All of these must be done for the strengthening of the church" (1 Cor. 14:26) (Packer, Tenney, and White 1995:544).

Community Life and Commitment

An overview of the first six chapters of Acts presents a group of new believers committed to one another and to the task of reaching others with the gospel. They cared for and supported each other during the good times (Acts 2-4), the bad times (Acts 5), and times of disagreement (Acts 6:1-7). The growth of the Early Church (Acts 2:47; 4:4, 33; 5:12-14; 6:7) shows how this new community attracted new converts[20] through the commitment of its members to preaching of the gospel and to one another.

---

[20] "When we preach the doctrine, the doctrine occupies the first place in our thought, and is in the foreground of our mind. When we preach Christ, the Person is in the foreground and occupies the first place in our mind. When we speak of preaching Christianity it is the system of doctrine and practice of which we are really thinking: when we speak of preaching Christ we are really thinking of the revelation of Christ. But the Person is greater than the doctrine and far exceeds it, and consequently, when we speak of preaching Christianity and pass from the thought of Christ to the thought of the doctrine, we pass from the reality itself to the shadow of the reality.

"When we fall into this error, we inevitably tend to make the acceptance of the shadow, the doctrine, the system, the aim and object of our work. In doing that we are doing something of which Christ spoke in very severe terms. To make converts to a doctrine is to make proselytes. The proselyte abandons one system of thought and practice for another; and to adopt a new system of thought and practice is not the way of salvation. The Christian convert is a convert not to a system of doctrine but to Christ. It is in Christ that he trusts, not in any system of doctrine or of morals. The difference between the work of the Judaizing zealot and the Christian missionary lies here: that the one sought a convert to his doctrine; the other seeks a convert to his Lord. . . . When we put doctrine in the first place, we are in danger of failing into exactly that error which Christ condemned" (Allen 1960:58).

One of the greatest example of commitment was that of the apostle Paul who faced many hardships yet remained true to the task of the proclamation of the gospel (2 Cor. 6:3-13; Rom. 8:35). Paul later encourages Timothy that a true disciple is one who will face hardship as he endured. He speaks of a Roman soldier whose single-minded purpose, rigorous discipline, and unquestioning commitment to his commanding officer portrays a person who is a servant of the gospel (2 Tim. 2:1-4). This commitment can be seen in its membership, baptism, and Lord's Supper.

Membership: The Initiation of Our New Identity

The members of the Early Church lived a lifestyle that greatly contrasted that of today's church.   Luke speaks of "added to their number" (Acts 2:41, 47) and "the number of disciples in Jerusalem increased rapidly" (Acts 6:7). The New Testament witnesses to the fact that these new believers had a formal understanding of what church membership involved since letters of commendation were sent from one church to another (1 Cor. 16:3; 2 Cor. 3:1; 3 Jn. 5-9).

Even though membership within the Early Church was less formalized, its members viewed their inclusion with high esteem. They did not live individualistic lives, but saw themselves as a vital part of the larger community (Acts 8:14-17; 18:24-27; Rom. 15:26-27). Even the thought of living self-sufficient, isolated lives was inconceivable in the Early Church, because each believer was intertwined with other members of the community of love (Grenz 1996:229). As the community of love is one so we must also as members of this community must function as one, united in love and purpose. In the Old Testament, excommunication was the worst fate individuals could suffer, since it severed them from their inheritance among God's people. Likewise, in the New Testament, the fellowship of believers severed their relationship with the offender, like they would a pagan or a tax collector (Mt. 18:17; 1 Cor. 5:13).

Baptism: The Affirmation of Our New Identity

"There is one body and one Spirit—just as you were called to one hope when you were called—one Lord, one faith, one baptism; one God and Father of all, who is over all and through all and in all" (Eph. 4:4-6).

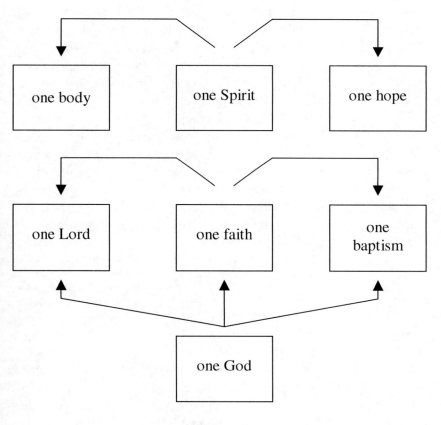

Figure 1

Sevenfold Unity of the Church
(Adapted from Hart 1999:483)

The purpose of Figure 1 is to describe the most important metaphor that the apostle Paul used for the Church: the body of Christ. Paul describes the body of Christ as a sevenfold unity of the Spirit as both a triad and a Trinity (Eph. 4:4ff). The term in the center of each triad is the key for each. In the first triad it is the "one Spirit" who creates the "one body" of believers and the "one hope" shared by both Jew and Gentile believers, which rests upon God's call and initiative. In the second triad it is "one faith" which unites all believers to "one Lord" and "one baptism" is the external affirmation of our faith in Jesus Christ. It is "one God and Father of all, who is over all and through all and in all," which forms the foundation for all.

Paul begins in the first triad by describing the "one body" as the body of Christ and each person is placed here at conversion by the Holy Spirit (1 Cor. 12:12-31). However, this "one body" does not excuse them from belonging to a local body of believers where they can exercise their spiritual gifts and edify others to spiritual growth. Paul then describes the "one Spirit" who indwells and unifies all believers as "one body." It is the indwelling work of the Holy Spirit to transform the life of each member to become more like Jesus. "One hope" refers to the return of our Lord Jesus Christ and the Holy Spirit is *We are all children of one family who serve, love, and edify one another in order to maintain* "the unity of the Spirit through the bond of peace." the assurance of this great promise (Eph. 1:13-14). Paul's emphasis here is that as the believer recognizes the existence of "one body," walks in "one Spirit" will hope in the return of our Lord and "Make every effort to keep the unity of the Spirit through the bond of peace" (Eph. 4:3).

In the second triad, Paul describes "one Lord" as being the Lord Jesus Christ Himself who gave us the greatest example of the Christian life, died for us, rose from the grave and will someday soon return for "one body." This "one faith" is settled body of truth given by Jesus Christ Himself to His Church. The

Early Church recognized the basic doctrine that they taught, guarded, and entrusted to others (2 Tim. 2:2). Paul states that all believers should agree on this "one faith" and to depart from "one faith" will bring disunity within the "one body." The "one baptism" spoken of here is that of being incorporated into the body of Christ and our new identity is affirmed through water baptism. Each of these terms were intended to create a "unity of the Spirit" within the body of Christ. Lastly, it is "one God" which emphasizes the unity of the believer in the family of God. We are all children of one family who serve, love, and edify one another in order to maintain "the unity of the Spirit through the bond of peace" (Eph. 4:3).

Even though baptism was a common event in the Early Church, its believers were not the first to implement this sacrament. It was when Gentiles converted to the Christian faith that the Jews would baptize them, which was a symbol of purification. Even though John the Baptist viewed baptism as an important aspect of his ministry the New Testament is unclear as to whether or not Jesus baptized His converts, except for one occasion.

> "After this, Jesus and his disciples went out into the Judean countryside, where he spent some time with them, and baptized. Now John also was baptizing at Aenon near Salim, because there was plenty of water, and people were constantly coming to be baptized" (Jn. 3:22-23).

This occurred just before the arrest and imprisonment of John the Baptist, where both John and Jesus were preaching and baptizing simultaneously.

The significance of baptism in the Early Church had several meanings: it symbolized a person's death to sin (Rom. 6:4; Gal. 2:12); the cleansing from sin (Acts 22:16; Eph. 5:26); and new life in Christ (Acts 2:41; Rom. 6:3). Like John's baptism, it was for early Christians an expression of repentance and faith (Acts 2:38, 41; 8:12f.; 16:14f., 33f.; 18:8; 19:2f.; cf. Heb. 6:1f.). Often an entire family would be baptized, which probably demonstrated a person's desire to consecrate everything within his household to the Lord (Packer, Tenney, and White 1995:545). Paul J. Achtemeier states,

> The interpretation of Christian baptism was fluid in the first century. At Corinth it was compared to Israel's exodus through the sea and its eating of the manna in the desert (1 Cor. 10:1-4). In other places it was compared with Noah's escape from God's wrath on sinners (1 Pet. 3:21). It was also compared with Jesus' death and resurrection; Christians symbolically die to their sins and former lives, a death they share with Christ, and are buried with him; as they rise from baptism in purity, they share the new life brought by Jesus' resurrection (Rom. 6:1-4). Hence baptism may be compared to a new birth (John 3:4-5) (1985:92).

Baptism was and is a vital part of the Early Church and the church today for several reasons: first of all, it is an affirmation of our new identity. In baptism we affirm that we believe that Jesus was crucified, buried and resurrected. It symbolizes our spiritual union with Jesus. We have died with Christ to the old sinful ways of life and are now raised with Him to a new life (Rom. 6:3-8). Paul is stating that by faith believers are "baptized (placed) into Christ" and therefore united and identified with Him. This spiritual reality is then graphically witnessed to and pictured by believers' baptism in water. Second, it also involves a transfer of commitment. Through baptism we are publicly declaring our surrender of all former allegiances to our old self ("in Adam") and announcing our allegiance to the new self ("in Christ").

> A person's entrance into God's freedom or salvation, while an existential affair, also marks their introduction into a wider community. Baptism, which dynamically embodies and effects this translation from one way of life to another, necessarily involves a transferal from one community to another, from that "in Adam" to that "in Christ" (Banks 1994:78).

Third, it seals an agreement with God and becomes a vital part of the fellowship who confess Jesus is Lord. "For we were all baptized by one Spirit into one body—whether Jews or Greeks, slave or free—and we were all given the one Spirit to drink" (1 Cor. 12:13). Our new identity is defined by our new community—the life, death, burial, and resurrection of Jesus. Fourth, it gives us a hope, since its focus is toward the future. This hope rests in the return of Jesus Christ and our complete transformation (glorification) (Rom. 8:11; 1 Cor. 15:51-57). Finally, baptism affects not only our lives, but the lives of the community. Baptism affects our commitment to fulfill the mandate of mutual edification. In water baptism we are reminded of our new birth, however, more than this, it is the beginning of our spiritual journey with the Lord. When we witness someone's baptism we are accepting the responsibility of discipling and nurturing this new believer and all who the Lord has placed under our care (Grenz 1996:234-238).

"For we were all baptized by one Spirit into one body—whether Jews or Greeks, slave or free— and we were all given the one Spirit to drink"

These new believers were rejoicing in what the Lord had done among them with the coming of the Holy Spirit. There was within this community a spirit of rejoicing and generosity, which affected those whom they came in contact with daily. This rejoicing and generosity[21], was contagious and resulted in "Those who accepted his message were baptized, about three thousand were added to their number that day" (2:41) and "the Lord added to their number daily those who were being saved" (2:47).

The Jews generally looked on baptism as a rite only for Gentile converts (i.e., proselytes), not for one born a Jew. It symbolized the break with one's Gentile past and the washing away of any defilement. So when the Jews accepted baptism in the name of

---

[21] "The Greek ἀφελότητι καρδίας may be rendered "generosity of heart"; cf. ἁπλότητι τῆς καρδίας in much the same sense in Ephesians 6:5 and Colossians 3:22" (Bruce 1988:74).

Jesus on hearing Peter's message, it was traumatic and significant for them in a way we in our mildly christianized culture have difficulty understanding (Gaebelein 1981, 9:286).

The Lord's Supper: The Reaffirmation of Our New Identity

"For I received from the Lord what I also passed on to you: The Lord Jesus, on the night he was betrayed, took bread, and when he had given thanks, he broke it and said, 'This is my body, which is for you; do this in remembrance of me.' In the same way, after supper he took the cup, saying, 'This cup is the new covenant in my blood; do this, whenever you drink it, in remembrance of me.' For whenever you eat this bread and drink this cup, you proclaim the Lord's death until he comes" (1 Cor. 11:23-26).

Baptism, as stated above, initiates us into the body of Christ and seals our identity in the fellowship with other believers. However, the Lord's Supper is to be repeated often, which reaffirms what occurred in baptism. The early Christians partook of the Lord's Supper as a symbolic act in observance of the Jewish Passover feast. The words "after supper" indicate that the Lord's Supper was originally a full meal, introduced by the blessing and breaking of the bread and concluded by the blessing and passing of the cup. Packer, Tenney, and White state,

In the Passover, Jews rejoiced that God had delivered them from their enemies and they looked expectantly to their future as God's children. In the Lord's Supper, Christians celebrated how Jesus had delivered them from sin and they expressed their hope for the day when Christ would return (1 Cor. 11:26).

At first, the Lord's Supper was an entire meal that Christians shared in their homes. Each guest brought a dish of food to the common table. The meal began with common prayer and the eating of small pieces from a single loaf of bread that represented Christ's broken body. The meal closed with another prayer and the sharing of a cup of wine, which represented Christ's shed blood (1995:544).

It was speculated that the early Christians were conducting secret meetings when they observed the Lord's Supper. In A.D.

100, the Roman Emperor Trajan outlawed these secret meetings, and the Christians began to observe the Lord's Supper during the Early morning worship service, open to the public (Packer, Tenney, and White 1995:544).

In the social world of that time, breaking bread with someone symbolized acceptance and mutual recognition. It was an offer of peace, trust, brotherhood, and forgiveness; sharing a table meant sharing life. Jesus accepted those whom society rejected. Jesus' response to the poor was that of divine love which He lived and taught and departed this same spirit of love to His disciples (Giles 1995:34).

When we commemorate the Lord's Supper we, first of all celebrate what God has done for us in the past in sending His Son Jesus "to seek and to save what was lost" (Lk. 19:10). Second, we are to follow Jesus' commands to "do this in remembrance of me" (1 Cor. 11:24). Third, we remember that Jesus fellowshipped with tax collectors, publicans, and sinners and welcomed them to join Him in the new community (Lk. 18:9-14).

Finally, the purpose of the Lord's Supper is to remember the life, crucifixion, death, burial, and resurrection of our Lord. It does not only bring to remembrance our past, but it speaks to us in the present as we celebrate His blood that was poured out on our behalf with the community. This celebration includes our Lord's fellowship not only with us as His body as He gives us forgiveness and a new life, but also our fellowship with Him.

Through the Lord's Supper we also celebrate our present community with each other within Christ's body. The one loaf symbolizes the oneness of the fellowship we share (1 Cor. 10:17). And our eating and drinking together reminds us that the foundation of our unity rests with our common communion with Christ (Grenz 1996:241).

The Lord's Supper speaks of the future. "I tell you, I will not drink of this fruit of the vine from now on until that day when I drink it anew with you in my Father's kingdom" (Mt.

26:29). Jesus is saying that "Just as the first Passover looks forward not only to deliverance but to settlement in the land, so also the Lord's Supper looks forward to deliverance and life in the consummated kingdom" (Gaebelein 1984, 8:539).

Jesus commands them to celebrate the Lord's Supper "until he comes" and will sit with His people at the messianic banquet (Lk. 22:16, 18, 29-30). Jesus calls His disciples to celebrate His life from the cross to the crown and the eternal life, which God has provided through His death and resurrection. The Lord's Supper is a vital part of the Christian life. It is an act of our will as we celebrate what the Lord has done for us. Through this sacrament we reaffirm our faith, re-envision our hope, declare once again the depth of our love for the Lord, and thank God for "such a great salvation" (Heb. 2:3), and His divine grace. It is also an act of God, through our participation, that the Holy Spirit reminds us of our new identity as children of God, our covenant with God and others as we share life together in the community of love (Grenz 1996:241).

The role the Holy Spirit plays in the Lord's Supper is to remind us to follow Christ and His forgiveness. The Holy Spirit *refreshes us* as we face temptation, failure, and sin. The Holy Spirit *encourages us* to utilize the divine resources of His power available each and every day. The Holy Spirit *motivates us* to wait in hopeful expectation of His soon return. The Lord's Supper also has ethical implications, which should remind us that we can serve no other gods (1 Cor. 10:18-22). The Lord's Supper symbolizes unity and concern for the welfare of other members of the community.

Table 5

The Lord's Supper
(Iverson and Asplund 1995:82-83)

A Time of Remembrance "Celebration"	"For I received from the Lord what I also passed on to you: The Lord Jesus, on the night he was betrayed, took bread, and when he had given thanks, he broke it and said, 'This is my body, which is for you; do this in remembrance of me.' In the same way, after supper he took the cup, saying, 'This cup is the new covenant in my blood; do this, whenever you drink it, in remembrance of me'" (1 Cor. 11:23-25).
A Time of Proclamation "Declaration"	"For whenever you eat this bread and drink this cup, you proclaim the Lord's death until he comes" (1 Cor. 11:26).
A Time of Self-Examination "Humility, Repentance and Cleansing"	"Therefore, whoever eats the bread or drinks the cup of the Lord in an unworthy manner will be guilty of sinning against the body and blood of the Lord. A man ought to examine himself before he eats of the bread and drinks of the cup. For anyone who eats and drinks without recognizing the body of the Lord eats and drinks judgment on himself. That is why many among you are weak and sick, and a number of you have fallen asleep. But if we judged ourselves, we would not come under judgment" (1 Cor. 11:27-31).
A Time of Blessing "Joy of the Lord"	"The cup of blessing which we bless, is it not the communion of the blood of Christ? The bread which we break, is it not the communion of the body of Christ?" (1 Cor. 10:16, NKJV).
A Time of Fellowship and Unity "Unity in the Spirit"	"Is not the cup of thanksgiving for which we give thanks a participation in the blood of Christ? Because there is one loaf, we, who are many, are one body, for we all partake of the one loaf" (1 Cor. 10:17).

Implications for Today's Church

"Going a little farther, he fell with his face to the ground and prayed, 'My Father, if it is possible, may this cup be taken from me. Yet not as I will, but as you will.' Then he returned to his disciples and found them sleeping. 'Could you men not keep watch with me for one hour?' he asked Peter. Watch and pray so that you will not fall into temptation. The spirit is willing, but the body is weak'" (Mt. 26:39-41).

E. M. Bounds states,

The entire life of a Christian soldier—its being, intention, implication, and action—are all dependent on its being a life of prayer. Without prayer—no matter what else he has—the Christian soldier's life will be feeble and ineffective. Without prayer—he is an easy prey for his spiritual enemies" (1984:118).

Jesus is calling His body to a new radical lifestyle of prayer. Richard Foster states,

Radical prayer refuses to let us stay on the fringes of life's great issues. It dares to believe that things can be different. Its aim is the total transformation of persons, institutions, and societies. Radical prayer, you see, is prophetic. . . . To clasp the hands in prayer is the beginning of an uprising against the disorder of the world (1992:243).

Prayer was something more than a ritual or something that needed to be done. It was the air they breathed, the water and food that sustains life, without these, life no longer exists. Prayer was not just another duty that needed to be performed or drudgery, but a delight to spend precious time with the Savior of their souls. The Early Church gave the greatest example patterned after Jesus Christ for us to follow. Larry Lea states,

Mirrored in that tragic scene is the plight of the church today. Jesus, our interceding High Priest, is praying; His disciples are sleeping; and Satan is winning contest after contest by *default*. It would be impossible to calculate the failures, the ruined reputations, the defeats, the broken homes and the other multiplied tragedies that could have been avoided if believers had prayed. It would be impossible to measure the destruction that could have been turned and the judgment that might have been averted if only God's people had taken the time to pray. I am guilty, and so are you (1987:5).

Jesus taught His disciples that prayer transforms and reshapes each and every area of life. It changes our heart so that the void that once possessed our heart and life is now filled with the life and presence and promises of the Almighty God. Prayer directs our lives so that priorities are established and maintained, His

Prayer was something more than a ritual or something that needed to be done. It was the air that they breathed, the water and food that sustains life, without these, life no longer exists.

provision becomes a daily occurrence in our lives. Prayer changes life from being mediocre to a new dimension of greater joy and fulfillment with the Lord and with others.

Prayer transformed these sleepy, discouraged disciples into a bold, determined and unified army that seized opportunities and turned their society and world upside down. The prayer life of the Early Church was not a frustrating, confusing, hit-or-miss powerless experience, but the foundation to their success of spreading the gospel. The following illustration sums up the necessity of prayer within the lives of God's people.

There is a story of a man in search of God who came to study at the feet of an old teacher. The sage brought this young man to a lake and led him out into shoulder-deep water. Putting his hands upon his pupil's head, he promptly pushed him under the water and held him there until the disciple, feeling he would surely drown, frantically repelled the old man's resistance. In shock and confusion the young man resurfaced. "What is the meaning of this?" he demanded, His teacher looked him in the eyes and said, "When you desire God as you desire life, you shall find Him." The question here is not only of desire but of survival. When Jesus is your life, you cannot go on without Him (Frangipane 1991:44).

May we once again obey the voice of the Lord and return to our first love and devotion. Prayer, as Jesus described it, involved everyone who confessed Him as Lord and Savior of their life, and likewise, prayer today must go beyond denominational and church boundaries to encompass *all* of God's people. It is time for God's people to rise up on their knees and conquer the land that God has already given them. It is not enough for each church to have an effective prayer life, it must include members of the body of Christ from every denomination and church within each city and nation. Only then will prayer once again become the active force within our cities that God intended from the beginning. "Yet I hold this against you: You have forsaken your first love. Remember the height from which you have fallen! Repent and do the things you did at first. If you do not repent, I will come to you and remove your lampstand from its place" (Rev. 2:4-5).

To the same degree that our Lord is calling His body to a life of prayer and devotion, He is also calling us to worship Him from hearts that desire intimacy with Him. Worship in the Early Church like prayer was an integral characteristic of their new life in Jesus Christ. Worship was transformed from being ritualistic to an inner lifestyle that glorified God and edified others. "Worship is an opportunity for man to invite God's power and presence to move among those worshiping Him" (Hayford 1987:53).

The Early Church knew and responded to this power and presence, which was the key along with prayer to effective ministry. They knew that worship and prayer were the keys to effective evangelism and the edification of the church. It was through worship they would find the Lord who created them for joy and be redeemed from everything that would hinder or destroy that joy. Through worship we acknowledge

God's great *love* for us, verified in His Son Jesus; God's great *forgiveness*, insuring acceptance before Him; God's great *purpose* in us, establishing worth and dignity; and God's great *promises* to us, giving confidence for tomorrow. Small wonder thousands of souls have opened their lives to Jesus in this atmosphere! (Hayford 1987:54).

The greatest benefit that we receive through worship is not the acknowledgement of the depth of our sin, our weakness, or the greatness of His grace and power, but will we allow the Holy Spirit to lead us before the throne of God and seek Him in Spirit and truth.

Jesus in the Beatitudes said, "Blessed are those who hunger and thirst for righteousness, for they will be filled" (Mt. 5:6). The Early Church knew that the foundation to godly living was to "hunger and thirst for righteousness." They also knew that the Christian's hunger for the things of God was hindered or even destroyed by worldly anxiety, deceitfulness of wealth (Mt. 13:22), desire for things (Mk. 4:19), and life's pleasures (Lk. 8:14), and failure to abide in Jesus Christ (Jn. 15:4).

When a Christian no longer hungers or thirsts after God and His righteousness, spiritual death occurs because it is the presence and power of God within our lives that truly gives us life. We live in a day where we must know and respond to our Lord and Savior with an insatiable hunger and thirst to be filled with His presence. In today's society, we are faced with an overwhelming hunger and thirst for unrighteousness as seen in Paul's second letter to Timothy.

> "But mark this: There will be terrible times in the last days. People will be lovers of themselves, lovers of money, boastful, proud, abusive, disobedient to their parents, ungrateful, unholy, without love, unforgiving, slanderous, without self-control, brutal, not lovers of the good, treacherous, rash, conceited, lovers of pleasure rather than lovers of God—having a form of godliness but denying its power. Have nothing to do with them" (2 Tim. 3:1-5).

It is time for the body of Christ to confront this spirit of unrighteousness with a true "hunger and thirst for righteousness" (Mt. 5:6).

Today's society is filled with relationships that lack commitment. Whether it is between a husband and wife, parents and children, commitment to one's vocation or profession, or the church they attend. Commitment has lost its affect on our lives and the lives of others. A person who is committed to a particular task or person is seen as something extraordinary, when it should be the norm. We have been called to be committed to a higher calling and the fulfillment of the Great Commission. The apostle Paul in his letter to the Ephesians instructs them "I urge you to live a life worthy of the calling you have received" (Eph. 4:1). Paul tells them that they have been called to a higher calling, which is accomplished by being "completely humble and gentle; be patient, bearing with one another in love" (Eph. 4:2).

When a Christian no longer hungers or thirsts after God and His righteousness, spiritual death occurs because it is the presence and power of God within our lives that truly gives us life.

The Greek word "worthy" ἀξίως *(axiōs)* means "equal weight" and refers to one's calling and Christian behavior should be balanced. "This calling" refers not only to the believers' salvation (cf. Rom. 1:5-6; 1 Cor. 1:9) but also to the unity of the Spirit that should exist within one body under Jesus Christ. Therefore, a Christian's behavior involves his personal life and responsibility to other believers in the church (Walvoord and Zuck 1983:632). Thoralf Gilbrant states, "*axiōs* denotes the proper way of receiving and sending (showing hospitality to) itinerant ministers of the gospel. . . . Paul warned those who might participate in the Lord's Supper 'unworthily'" (1986, 11:313).

All believers have been baptized into "one body." Jesus never intended that His body would be severed into thousands of denominations and/or churches. He intended that every believer would become a vital part of His body. "One baptism" answers the questions, "who am I?" and "where do I belong?"

It places the new believer in the body of Christ where they come to know who they are in Jesus Christ and also gives them a sense of belonging and security. This lack has caused many new believers to fall away from the faith instead of being incorporated into active church life.

As baptism affirms our new identity through incorporation into the body of Christ, the Lord's Supper reaffirms our new identity through continual remembrance of what Jesus accomplished on our behalf on the cross. Sharing the Lord's Supper and a meal symbolized oneness, acceptance, and mutual edification. The Early Church realized that true life did not exist without sharing the Lord's Supper and sharing a meal. This naturally resulted in the proclamation of the gospel as non-believers were drawn into the church because of the unity of the Spirit that existed between the members.

As we partake in the Lord's Supper and consider Christ's precious sufferings, let us also examine our discernment of His body, the church. Do we love the least of our brothers and sisters in our fellowship? Do we harbor grudges or unforgiveness? Do we know the body of Christ in our neighboring congregations? Do we esteem them and love them as a part of the family of God? Jesus said they are His body—they are the great treasure for which He traded His life, they are in whom He dwells by His Spirit. Whatever value we place upon them, is the value we place upon Christ.

The church today must realize that unity of the Spirit must exist in every area of life within the body of Christ and not just those that feel most comfortable to us. These differences must be dealt with through getting to know what other denominations believe, their focus of ministry and come together in prayer and fasting, celebrating the Lord's Supper, ministry and outreach. Only when Jesus is "lifted up from the earth" will our communities see the true Church that Jesus established (Jn. 12:32).

Chapter 4

Leadership in the
Early Church

The purpose of this chapter is to describe the characteristics and influence that leadership within the Early Church had upon its members and the role of women within its structure. It presents the function of leadership within the community life of the Early Church and its function within the church today.

> "Paul and Barnabas appointed elders for them in each church and, with prayer and fasting, committed them to the Lord, in whom they had put their trust" (Acts 14:23).

Paul and Barnabas knew that in order to strengthen the churches they had planted, they needed to appoint elders or leaders in each church. Through the guidance and direction of the Holy Spirit they discerned which members had attained sufficient degree of spiritual maturity to serve their fellow believers. They also knew that these leaders could instruct and encourage these fellow believers to face hardship, persecution and maintain their Christian witness. "Rather than inheriting leadership, the house church structure imparted, through the hosts, actual leadership which in turn determined the form of church life (cf. 1 Cor. 16:16)" (Birkey 1988:59). Paul was admonishing the Corinthian believers to accept and submit to the leadership of Stephanas who was the owner of this household church, but also to those who were a part of his household church.

The Synagogue

Leadership within the synagogue was not the responsibility of the priests, but of lay officials and a council of elders directed by a "synagogue ruler" (Mk. 5:22), who was in charge of the worship, building maintenance, congregational discipline. This synagogue ruler would sometimes require the help of an attendant (Lk. 4:20), who would administer discipline (Lk. 13:14). The apostle Paul was often disciplined by Jewish attendants (2 Cor. 11:24-29) (Matthews 1995:260).

Two Types of Leadership

There are two types of leadership: the first is worldly leadership which Ted Engstrom states, "Authority is whatever you possess at the moment that causes someone else to do what you want him to do at the moment" (1976:112). The assumption here is that the goal of the leader is to cause those who follow to do his or her will, and not necessarily God's will. The second is Christian leadership as J. Robert Clinton states,

> Leadership is technically defined as a dynamic process over an extended period of time in which a leader (utilizing leadership resources and by specific leadership behaviors) influences the thoughts and activities of followers, toward accomplishment of aims—usually mutually beneficial for leaders, followers, and the macro-context of which they are a part. . . . It is also a process in which a man or woman with God-given capacity influences a specific group of God's people toward His purposes for the group (1988:14, 245).

The Foundation of Leadership: To Love One Another

> "Jesus replied: 'Love the Lord your God with all your heart and with all your soul and with all your mind.' This is the first and greatest commandment. And the second is like it: 'Love your neighbor as yourself.' All the Law and the Prophets hang on these two commandments" (Mt. 22:37-40).

Love for God and one another is the very essence, heart, goal, and substance of Scripture. "A new command I give you: Love one another. As I have loved you, so you must love one another" (Jn. 13:34; 15:12, 17). These two commands sum up

God's commands in Scripture. Loving and caring for one another is not an option for the Christian. It is a mandate and a solid proof of our love for the Lord and our fellowship with Him. Love for God and our neighbor becomes our source and means of obedience in the other imperatives of Scripture by virtue of internal motives and the inner ability to carry out God's commands through the power of His love operating in us by the ministry of His Spirit (cf. Gal. 5:22; 1 Th. 4:2-9).

Without the reality of these two commands in our lives as both source and course, derivation and destination, obedience to Scripture will become merely legalistic. The legal demands become burdens that we seek to obey to gain points with God and with men, and all our works and ministries naturally become acts of self-love. They are things we do for praise, power, position, or to feel better about ourselves.

Throughout Scripture we can see how the phrase "one another" was a very important role in the message and life of the New Testament. The one another commands of Scripture fall into two categories, those concerned with the progress of spiritual growth and those concerned with the process of spiritual regression and fall out.

Love for God and our neighbor becomes our source and means of obedience in the other imperatives of Scripture by virtue of internal motives and the inner ability to carry out God's commands through the power of His love operating in us by the ministry of His Spirit.

Table 6

The Process of Spiritual Growth

Love one another	"A new command I give you: Love one another. As I have loved you, so you must love one another" (Jn. 13:34).
Members of one another	"So we, being many, are one body in Christ, and individually members of one another" (Rom. 12:5, NKJV; Eph. 4:25).
Peace with one another	"Salt is good, but if it loses its saltiness, how can you make it salty again? Have salt in yourselves, and be at peace with each other" (Mk. 9:50).
Devoted to one another	"Be devoted to one another in brotherly love" (Rom. 12:10).
Honor one another	"Honor one another above yourselves" (Rom. 12:10).
Live in harmony with one another	"Live in harmony with one another" (Rom. 12:16; 15:5).
Accept one another	"Accept one another, then, just as Christ accepted you, in order to bring praise to God" (Rom. 15:7).
Instruct one another	"I myself am convinced, my brothers, that you yourselves are full of goodness, complete in knowledge and competent to instruct one another" (Rom. 15:14).
Greet one another	"Greet one another with a holy kiss" (Rom. 16:16).
Wait for one another	"Therefore, my brethren, when you come together to eat, wait for one another" (1 Cor. 11:33, NKJV).
Same care for one another	"That there should be no schism in the body, but that the members should have the same care for one another" (1 Cor. 12:25, NKJV).

Serve one another	"You, my brothers, were called to be free. But do not use your freedom to indulge the sinful nature; rather, serve one another in love" (Gal. 5:13).
Bearing with one another	"Be completely humble and gentle; be patient, bearing with one another in love" (Eph. 4:2).
Kind to one another	"And be kind to one another, tenderhearted," (Eph. 4:32, NKJV).
Forgiving one another	"Forgiving one another, just as God in Christ forgave you" (Eph. 4:32, NKJV).
Speak to one another	"Speak to one another with psalms, hymns and spiritual songs. Sing and make music in your heart to the Lord" (Eph. 5:19).
Submit to one another	"Submit to one another out of reverence for Christ" (Eph. 5:21).
Comfort one another	"Therefore comfort one another with these words" (1 Th. 4:18, NKJV).
Edify one another	"Therefore comfort each other and edify one another, just as you also are doing" (1 Th. 5:11, NKJV).
Consider one another	"And let us consider one another in order to stir up love and good works," (Heb. 10:24, NKJV).
Exhorting one another	"Not forsaking the assembling of ourselves together, as is the manner of some, but exhorting one another, and so much the more as you see the Day approaching" (Heb. 10:25, NKJV).
Confess your trespasses to one another	"Confess your trespasses to one another . . . that you may be healed" (Jas. 5:16, NKJV).
Pray for one another	"Pray for one another, that you may be healed" (Jas. 5:16).
Live in harmony	"Finally, all of you, live in harmony with one another; be sympathetic, love as brothers, be

with one another	compassionate and humble" (1 Pet. 3:8).
Offer hospitality to one another	"Offer hospitality to one another without grumbling" (1 Pet. 4:9).

The process of spiritual growth can only be carried out when we allow the Holy Spirit to guide and direct our lives and are filled with the love of God. Without the influence of the Holy Spirit, we will become indifferent to the needs of others, dominated by the deeds of the flesh, and seek to meet our own needs for significance, praise, and the applause of men at the expense of others (cf. 1 Tim. 1:5).

However, in the process of spiritual regression, as seen in Table 7, we find hindrances to loving one another, hindrances to fellowship. We also find hindrances to nurturing one another, which is the function of the leader, and training others to do likewise. As we nurture one another, the body of Christ is built up and become mature in the Lord. These negative commands stress and point to what we naturally tend to do without the transforming life and power of the Lord, the ministry of the Holy Spirit, a daily life of prayer, and daily renewal in the Word operating within our lives continually.

Table 7

The Process of Spiritual Regression

Do not accept praise from one another	"How can you believe if you accept praise from one another, yet make no effort to obtain the praise that comes from the only God?" (Jn. 5:44).
Do not judge one another	"Therefore let us stop passing judgment on one another. Instead, make up your mind not to put any stumbling block or obstacle in your brother's way" (Rom 14:13).
Do not go to law against one another	"Now therefore, it is already an utter failure for you that you go to law against one another. Why do you not rather accept wrong? Why do you not rather *let yourselves* be cheated?" (1 Cor. 6:7, NKJV).
Do not be consumed by one another	"But if you bite and devour one another, beware lest you be consumed by one another!" (Gal. 5:15, NKJV).
Do not bite and devour one another	"But if you bite and devour one another, beware lest you be consumed by one another!" (Gal. 5:15, NKJV).
Do not provoke one another	"Let us not become conceited, provoking and envying one another" (Gal. 5:26).
Do not envy one another	"Let us not become conceited, provoking and envying one another" (Gal. 5:26).
Do not lie to one another	"Do not lie to one another, since you have put off the old man with his deeds" (Col. 3:9, NKJV).
Do not hate one another	"At one time we too were foolish, disobedient, deceived and enslaved by all kinds of passions and pleasures. We lived in malice and envy, being hated and hating one another" (Tit. 3:3).
Do not slander one another	"Brothers, do not slander one another. Anyone who speaks against his brother or judges him speaks against the law and judges it. When you

	judge the law, you are not keeping it, but sitting in judgment on it" (Jas. 4:11).
Do not grumble Against one another	"Do not grumble against one another, brethren, lest you be condemned. Behold, the Judge is standing at the door!" (Jas. 5:9, NKJV).

Those who have been called to be leaders within the body of Christ are to set the example "for the believers in speech, in life, in love, in faith and in purity" (1 Tim. 4:12). Paul instructed the Corinthians to "Follow my example, as I follow the example of Christ" (1 Cor. 11:1). Paul also told the Thessalonians that "for you yourselves are taught by God to love one another" (1 Th. 4:9, NKJV) since "love comes from God" (1 Jn. 4:7), "we also ought to love one another" (1 Jn. 4:11).

The Function of Leadership: To Nurture One Another

"It was he who gave some to be apostles, some to be prophets, some to be evangelists, and some to be pastors and teachers, to prepare God's people for works of service, so that the body of Christ may be built up until we all reach unity in the faith and in the knowledge of the Son of God and become mature, attaining to the whole measure of the fullness of Christ" (Eph. 4:11-13).

The Book of Ephesians is the only writing in the New Testament that the word "church" meant the church universal rather than the local church. Paul saw the church on two levels: first, as the body of Christ, made up of all true believers, growing until it reaches spiritual maturity. Second, as the local body of believers ministering to each other, growing together and experiencing spiritual unity. Ephesians 4:11-16 is one of the most important passages for understanding what God's plan is for individuals and churches.

The Lord provides communicators with spiritual gifts, which enable them to teach us God's word with insight and accuracy. It is the outline of a believer's growth from spiritual childhood to maturity, from being a victim of today's crisis to being victorious with Jesus Christ on the battlefield of spiritual warfare. The church, a body of learning, growing, functioning saints, enables its own edification by the coordinated functioning of mature individuals who provide the saints with the example for them to follow.

Leadership is described in Scripture as a gift of the Holy Spirit (Rom. 12:8). However, it is not based upon a particular personality type since this would limit those who could be leaders. New Testament leadership can be marked by specific virtues as demonstrated by: Peter whose style of leadership was based on his personal strength (Acts 4:8-12). James demonstrated the virtue of practical wisdom (Acts 15:12-21), and Paul through intellectual capacity, which was seen in his sermons and epistles. Timothy was a leader of sacrificial service (Phil. 2:19-21), and John by virtue of his heart for God and man (as seen in his writings). All these leaders shared all these virtues, but each of them had a distinct personality strength that uniquely marked him. This demonstrates the fact that leadership is not a matter of human personality but of

> *The church, a body of learning, growing, functioning saints, enables its own edification by the coordinated functioning of mature individuals who provide the saints with the example for them to follow.*

divine sovereignty. Just as the Spirit's gifts are not reserved for a few outstanding people so the Spirit's gift of leadership is not reserved for a particular kind of personality.

The gift of leadership is discovered and developed in the same way as other spiritual gifts, that is, through life experience, training, and the maturing process. Even though it is the product of the Spirit's presence and God's grace, this gift requires diligence, faithfulness, hard work, and commitment if it is to be exercised effectively.

In the New Testament, Paul's primary concern was to see the body of Christ built up and become mature in the Lord (Col.

1:28-2:2). Encouraging and building up refer to the process of building spiritual maturity and Christian character through the function of the various gifts of believers—particularly teaching and the encouragement of others. Each believer is to be involved in the edification process of the church, the building up of one another, which is figurative of the process of spiritual strengthening and edification. The primary importance is the spiritual health of one another.

The most important thing for all of us is our walk with the Lord. The one another commands of Scripture are a means to an end—ministry to one another with the goal of Christ-likeness through helping others to experience the sufficiency of the Savior. But one individual can only do so much, and God's strategy is for the body of Christ to be involved in this same concern for all members of the body "so we, being many, are one body in Christ, and individually members of one another" (Rom. 12:5, NKJV). Lois Barrett states,

> When we nurture one another, we help each other become what God calls us to be. Discovery includes all the ways we learn of God and God's activity in the world. And training, or guidance, helps us act out our discipleship in the world around us (1986:72).

As the body of Christ, we are to "love one another deeply, from the heart" (1 Pet. 1:22), and not to "love with words or tongue but with actions and in truth," for "this is how we know what love is: Jesus Christ laid down his life for us. And we ought to lay down our lives for our brothers" (1 Jn. 3:16, 18). John here is describing the nature of love, which demonstrates for us that just as Jesus submitted Himself

This "greater love" *culminates in (15:12-13), where Jesus emphasizes that true love submits oneself to others, places others before oneself, and ultimately gives their life for another. True love gives everything, which is the greatest proof of love.*

to the will of His Father, we are likewise to submit ourselves to one another.

The Greeks viewed submission as doing what is best for another person. For example, if two men were in a war, and one man was going to be shot and killed, the other man would submit himself to him by stepping in front of his friend and die in his place. Jesus exemplified submission when He submitted Himself to humankind by giving His life on the cross. Jesus commands His disciples to do likewise, "My command is this: Love each other as I have loved you. Greater love has no one than this, that he lay down his life for his friends" (Jn. 15:12-13). Jesus had stressed the attitude and duty of love towards His disciples earlier in the gospel of John (14:15, 21, 23, 28). This "greater love" culminates in (15:12-13), where Jesus emphasizes that true love submits oneself to others, places others before oneself, and ultimately gives their life for another. True love gives everything, which is the greatest proof of love. It is said that just before the apostle John passed away, he was carried from place to place and all he could say was "brothers, love one another." The word "love" is used forty-two times in the three Epistles of John and the phrase "love one another" is used six times (1 Jn. 3:11, 23; 4:7, 11-12; 2 Jn. 5).

> "The reason my Father loves me is that I lay down my life—only to take it up again. No one takes it from me, but I lay it down of my own accord. I have authority to lay it down and authority to take it up again. This command I received from my Father" (Jn. 10:17-18).

> "This is how we know what love is: Jesus Christ laid down his life for us. And we ought to lay down our lives for our brothers" (1 Jn. 3:16).

The Identity of Leadership: To Serve One Another

> "Jesus called them together and said, 'You know that those who are regarded as rulers of the Gentiles lord it over them, and their high officials exercise authority over them. Not so with you. Instead,

whoever wants to become great among you must be your servant, and whoever wants to be first must be slave of all. For even the Son of Man did not come to be served, but to serve, and to give his life as a ransom for many'" (Mk. 10:42-45).

There are four classes of Greek words to describe servanthood. The first is δουλεύω *(douleúō)*, and means "to be subject to another's will as a slave," "to serve." The second is διακονέω *(diakonéō)*, and means "to serve," "to aid," "to act as a deacon." "It incorporates every kind of ministry to persons and involves the full exercise of the gifts and abilities each of us has for the benefit of others in the body of Christ" (Richards 1985:551). "Each one should use whatever gift he has received to serve others, faithfully administering God's grace in its various forms" (1 Pet. 4:10). The third is λειτουργέω *(leitourgéō)*, which means "to serve as a priest in worship rituals." "In Greek culture it referred to community service. In Judaism, it focused specifically on the religious service of the priest and Levite." The fourth is λατρεύω *(latreúō)*, and means "to serve in a religious sense," "to worship," or "to serve God" (Richards 1985:552).

"Each one should use whatever gift he has received to serve others, faithfully administering God's grace in its various forms."

Jesus gave us the greatest example of being a servant, from both the Old Testament[22] and New Testament. James and John and possibly the other disciples were still thinking that Jesus was going to establish an earthly kingdom, even though He had just made it clear that he would suffer and die and be resurrected on the third day. They were trying to influence Jesus to give them places that only God could bestow. Jesus rebukes them for trying to destroy the unity and community among themselves and tells them that greatness is achieved by humble service.

---

[22] See Appendix B.

Jesus set an example of servanthood when He chose to empty Himself, become powerless, or to be emptied of significance (Phil. 2:5-8). He literally became poor as a servant, which stresses His voluntary submission of His glory with the wealth derived from others through His gracious act of giving. "For you know the grace of our Lord Jesus Christ, that though he was rich, yet for your sakes he became poor, so that you through his poverty might become rich" (2 Cor. 8:9).

Jesus called His disciples to serve, which is the most important characteristic of the Christian life. However, if serving is not based on love "I am only a resounding gong or a clanging cymbal. . . . I am nothing" (1 Cor. 13:1-3). The primary purpose for our existence is to glorify God and to express His love in a world without His love, which is accomplished through being a servant.

> In Greek thought, both types of service were shameful. The duty of the Greek person was to himself, to achieve his potential for excellence. To be forced to subject his will or surrender his time and efforts for the sake of others was intensely distasteful, even humiliating (Richards 1985:551).

However, Jesus said, "For even the Son of Man did not come to be served, but to serve, and to give his life as a ransom for many" (Mk. 10:45). Through this example, Jesus established a pattern that would transform the value system of His day. Serving brought complete fulfillment to the lifestyle of the Greeks and through living after Jesus' example we can achieve our full potential by giving, not by demanding (Richards 1985:551).

The Method of Leadership: To Teach One Another

> "Watch your life and doctrine closely. Persevere in them, because if you do, you will save both yourself and your hearers" (1 Tim. 4:16).

Paul instructs Timothy concerning the basis of a servant-leader's power to influence, which is his integrity "watch your life" and his reputation "you will save both yourself and your hearers." We lead others to the extent that we influence them. What better influence could Timothy have than the apostle Paul? Too often we try to preserve our reputation, but in doing so we end up loosing our integrity. However, if we watch our integrity, God will watch our reputation, which was the lesson that Paul was teaching Timothy, through his own experience (1 Cor. 9:27). Paul's instruction to Timothy, first of all, focused on his inner thought, feelings, motivation, and attitude, then on his outward ministry of teaching sound doctrine.

> *We lead others to the extent that we influence them. Too often we try to preserve our reputation, but in doing so we end up loosing our integrity. However, if we watch our integrity, God will watch our reputation, which was the lesson that Paul was teaching Timothy, through his own experience (1 Cor. 9:27).*

Paul demonstrated to Timothy, through integrity and reputation, that the basis for a servant-leader's influence is the reality of the Word of God, expressed through lifestyle and teaching. "Let the word of Christ dwell in you richly as you teach and admonish one another with all wisdom, and as you sing psalms, hymns and spiritual songs with gratitude in your hearts to God" (Col. 3:16). Paul was teaching Timothy that the basic qualification for spiritual leaders has nothing to do with personal gifting, spiritual gifting, training, or experience.

The affirmation of public and visible leadership is good, but it misses the main point stressed in the New Testament. Leadership is not so much to be public in its activity as in its character. It is the character, values, attitudes, behavior, and commitment of the leaders, as these reflect Christlikeness, that provide the compelling model (Richards and Hoeldtke 1980:117).

Gifted leaders are those who are a living demonstration of the reality of what they teach. It is not enough to practice what we preach. A true gifted leader will preach what they practice.

Teaching is an important aspect of Christian leadership (cf. 1 Tim. 3:2, "able to teach"). The apostles persisted in it with enthusiasm and faithfulness: "And every day, in the temple and from house to house, they kept right on teaching and preaching Jesus as the Christ" (Acts 5:42). The same concern for teaching and discipleship is evident in the ministry of Paul and Barnabas at Antioch (Acts 11:26; 15:35; cf. 13:1) and in Paul's lengthy teaching sessions in Corinth (Acts 18:11) and Ephesus (Acts 19:8-10; 20:31). Philip and Apollos are also cited as effective teachers (Acts 8:26-39; 18:27-28). The strengthening of the churches was important to Luke, and absolutely indispensable to genuine long-term church growth.

The Goal of Leadership: To Edify One Another

> "For God did not appoint us to wrath, but to obtain salvation through our Lord Jesus Christ, who died for us, that whether we wake or sleep, we should live together with Him. Therefore comfort each other and edify one another, just as you also are doing" (1 Th. 5:9-11).

Paul's focus here is encouraging the Thessalonians to "be alert and self-controlled" (v. 6), and that as the coming of the Lord draws closer, it must inspire His people to live together in harmony, and in eager expectation. Paul uses the two imperatives "to comfort or encourage each other," which literally means "to build a house" and signifies a habitual action, and the idea of strengthening one another by one's word(s); and "edify one another," which promotes spiritual growth through strengthening one another, especially those who are weak in faith (Morris 1991:162).

The goal of the Christian leader is "to bring others, and the whole local body, to a responsive relationship with Jesus Christ. Our goal is to help others seek, come to know, and to do His will" (Richards and Hoeldtke 1980:138). Worldly leadership seeks power and control as a means of accomplishing a task. However, in contrast to this, Christian leadership seeks no power, but speaks and acts with a God-given authority, which is based on God's love. Too often the issue of power and control is used within the church, which results in the body of Christ being torn down and not built up, or edified.

> "This is why I write these things when I am absent, that when I come I may not have to be harsh in my use of authority—the authority the Lord gave me for building you up, not for tearing you down" (2 Cor. 13:10).

The task of leadership within the church today is to set free its members from bondage and edify them so that each one will be personally responsible to Jesus. Even though, the Lord had given Paul the authority "for building you up," he was also given the authority necessary to confront and discipline moral offenders as in the case of the immoral brother (1 Cor. 5:1-13). James needed to confront a spirit of strife, "envy and selfish ambition" (3:14), which was causing division among the brethren. James begins and ends chapter four by describing the sins of the tongue and the failure to control the tongue is a form of self-righteous pride.

The goal of the Christian leader is *"to bring others, and the whole local body, to a responsive relationship with Jesus Christ. Our goal is to help others seek, come to know, and to do His will."*

James also confronted their self-confident boasting and refers to them as a "mist that appears for a little while and then vanishes" (Jas. 4:14). James is speaking to Christians who had become slanderers, who were criticizing and judging one another, and therefore, destroying their unity and their community lifestyle. In judging one another, they were placing themselves above the law and declaring that the law was an unnecessary statute. Rather than submitting to the law and obeying its statutes, they were declaring it to be invalid and useless (Gaebelein 1981, 12:196). Spiritual leaders have not been lifted above other Christians to judge their lifestyle and behavior. We have been called to judge ourselves (Mt. 7:1-6; 1 Cor. 11:27-29). James was confronting a very serious sin that was spreading quickly among the brethren. Adamson states,

Indeed the rabbis taught that judging our neighbor logically leads to a graver sin of judging God: Rabbi Asi declared that the man who begins disavowing his neighbor will end by denying God. We must be careful to note the far-reaching consequences of James's teaching here: respect for law and order is necessary for the health of modern society, but James goes on to remind us (v. 12) that, since God is the source of the law, what is ultimately at stake in a "permissive society" is respect for the authority of God himself. . . judge not your neighbor before you find yourself in the same situation (1976:177).

Edifying Discipline

"Those who oppose him he must gently instruct, in the hope that God will grant them repentance leading them to a knowledge of the truth, and that they will come to their senses and escape from the trap of the devil, who has taken them captive to do his will" (2 Tim. 2:25-26).

"All Scripture is God-breathed and is useful for teaching, rebuking, correcting and training in righteousness, so that the man of God may be thoroughly equipped for every good work" (2 Tim. 3:16).

Discipline in the church is not punishment. Discipline is designed to train and restore. In the New Testament the Greek word παιδεία (paideía) relates to the upbringing of children, who need direction, teaching, instruction, and discipline. Both the way of education and the goal are indicated by paideía.

The Jewish tradition comes in contact with the broader educational ideal of Greece. In the world of the Greeks these terms were applied to the household training of children and also to man's training to take his place in the culture of the world—with little emphasis on chastisement (Buttrick 1962, 1:846).

The edification process is designed to build up believers so they can be conformed to the image and character of Christ. Church discipline as a part of the edification process ministers to those within the body of Christ who are dominated by some area of sin so they can experience liberation from its power through fellowship with Christ. Jay E. Adams states that discipline

> functions in the educational process to produce righteousness as its fruit. Righteousness (rightness; conformity to Christ's standard of conduct) has the flavor of peace because, wherever it is found, it produces harmony and order. Where there is conformity to God's will, there is structure; where there is biblical structure the prime condition for learning is present: peace . . . where there is no peace, there is no learning; where there is no discipline, there is no order; where there is no order there is no peace. Discipline is, at its heart and core, good order (1986:14).

Without peace, learning is impossible because education depends upon order. When peace is lacking, there is poor learning in our schools and in our churches. Children, adolescence, and adults have a harder time to concentrate when there is a lack of peace. This is the same problem that James confronted "For where you have envy and selfish ambition, there you find disorder and every evil practice" (Jas. 3:16).

Dean S. Gilliland states,

> The purpose of discipline, therefore, is to bring both restoration of the errant person and healing to the entire fellowship. It is just as important focus on the group as it is on the individual. The tendency to judge the individual alone violates the principle of the oneness of the body of Christ. The defection of anyone is a corporate failure (1998:244).

Gilliland includes not only the offender, but the congregation, is always affected. He views church discipline as a holistic ministry, which includes family, friends, and the entire body of believers. He also states "discipline, carefully administered, is a means of teaching the individual and the group what the standards of the Christian life are" (1998:244). The purpose of discipline within the Early Church was:

- To bring glory to God and enhance the testimony of the people of God.
- To produce a healthy faith, one sound in doctrine (Tit. 1:13; 1 Tim. 1:19-20).
- To restore, heal, and build up sinning believers (Mt. 18:15; 2 Th. 3:14-15; Heb. 12:10-13; Gal. 6:1-2; Jas. 5:20).
- To win a soul to Christ, if the sinning person is only a professing Christian (2 Tim. 2:24-26).
- To silence false teachers and their influence in the church (Tit. 1:10-11).
- To set an example for the rest of the body and promote godly fear (1 Tim. 5:20).
- To protect the church against the destructive consequences that occur when churches fail to carry out church discipline.

Women in the Early Church[23]

"You are all sons of God through faith in Christ Jesus, for all of you who were baptized into Christ have clothed yourselves with Christ. There is neither Jew nor Greek, slave nor free, male nor female, for you are all one in Christ Jesus. If you belong to Christ, then you are Abraham's seed, and heirs according to the promise" (Gal. 3:26-29).

The apostle Paul is all-inclusive in his letters to the churches, rather than to any particular person or group within the church. Paul uses phrases like "When you are assembled" as a church (1 Cor. 5:4), "So if the whole church comes

---

[23] Due to the nature of this book, controversial subjects concerning women will not be discussed.

together" (1 Cor. 14:23) to stress that he is referring to both genders and not just men only. He also uses terms such as "all,"[24] "whoever" (1 Cor. 11:27), "everyone" (12:6), "anyone,"[25] and "each one"[26] to include both male and female. Therefore, in Paul's letters, both genders participate and contribute to the edification and welfare of community life (Banks 1994:119).

Women, according to Paul, made valuable contributions to the church as a whole. The congregation of the Early Church consisted primarily of women, which in the Roman upper class, more women had converted to Christianity than men. Even though they were not a part of the twelve disciples, women had an incredible influence in the Early Church. They followed Jesus and were more committed to Him at times than some of the disciples.

> At the cross it is women who stand around Jesus, not men, for they have all fled. It is not the disciples who first go to Jesus' grave, but the women. And the risen Lord first appears not to the disciples but to the women. There can be no doubt about all of this, for the simple fact that this tradition has been preserved for us indicates its factualness. The early period was definitely not an age that was friendly toward women, and these reports were preserved only because people could not do away with this old and fixed tradition. . . . In the New Testament we find women not only in serving roles, such as the deaconesses in Rom. 16:1, but also in the administration of the churches, even when men are available for these positions (Mk. 16:1-3) (Aland 1985:61, 63).

Jesus included women in His parables and teaching illustrations, which made it clear that His message and mission involved them. Therefore, Jesus honored women, showing equality between men and women. After the resurrection the

---

[24] 1 Cor. 10:17; 12:26; 14:5, 18, 23, 24, 31, NKJV.

[25] 1 Cor. 11:29, 34; 14:9, 16, 27, 37-38.

[26] Rom. 14:5; 1 Cor. 3:10; 7:17, 20; 12:7, 11, 27; 16:2; 2 Cor. 5:10; Gal. 6:4-5; Eph. 4:7; 5:33.

women "joined together constantly in prayer" with the other followers of Jesus, in complete fellowship with them (Acts 1:14). They helped to elect Matthias (Acts 1:15-26), and received the power and gifts of the Holy Spirit on the Day of Pentecost (Acts 2:1-4, 18).

It was in the home of Mary, the mother of John Mark, where the church in Jerusalem assembled (Acts 12:12), and Paul's first convert and congregation in Europe originated in the home of a woman—Lydia (Acts 16:13-15). It was Priscilla and Aquila who taught Apollos the "way of God more adequately" (Acts 18:24-26). Priscilla and Aquila are mentioned several times in Acts and the Pauline Epistles and each time it is Priscilla who is the predominant figure. She also played a leading role in the church, and with Aquila taught the disciples in Ephesus.

The congregation of the Early Church consisted primarily of women, which in the Roman upper class, more women had converted to Christianity than men.

Philip had four daughters that prophesied (Acts 21:9), and Paul mentions women who prophecy, which he considered the most important spiritual gift (1 Cor. 14:1-5). Paul mentions Phoebe who was "a servant of the church in Cenchrea" who was active in the ministry of the gospel (Rom. 16:1). He also mentions Nympha "and the church in her house" (Col. 4:15) who must have been an important part of Paul's ministry since Paul specifically mentions her by name (Douglas 1962:1259).

Implications for Today's Church

"For by the grace given me I say to every one of you: Do not think of yourself more highly than you ought, but rather think of yourself with sober judgment, in accordance with the measure of faith God has given you. Just as each of us has one body with many members, and these members do not all have the same function, so in Christ we who are many form one body, and each member belongs to all the others" (Rom. 12:3-5).

Throughout this chapter we have examined the primary characteristics of church leadership and the necessity of implementing them into our lives and ministry. After devoting eleven chapters to theological discussion, Paul now turns to an explanation of how this theology works out in daily living. He exhorts the readers to dedicate themselves to obedience to God, and that obedience is to be motivated by this theology (12:1). His exhortation is that they not be captivated by the foolishness of the world (1:21), but will, through the wisdom of God, become pure and mature (12:2).

In verses 3-8, Paul gives three practical examples of how the wisdom of God should affect one's life. The individual should be characterized by *meekness* as he recognizes that his salvation is the result of the grace of God. His meekness should result in smooth assimilation into the *membership* of the body of Christ, which results in opportunities for *ministry*, for the benefit of other members in the body. Paul has shown a natural progression of how leadership should function within the church and the body of Christ. Paul demonstrated that spiritual gifts are endowments of power that enable us to carry out the vital functions of body life in Christ as members of His body. These endowments are a supernatural enablement so that supernatural results are produced.

The apostle Paul addresses the issue that the Greeks were too individualistic and divisive and it was the norm for them to do as they pleased. The Greeks in general were proud and considered anyone who was not Greek as a barbarian, which created problems for Paul as he sought to establish a church among the Greeks. This same problem has existed within the church since the beginning and is one of the greatest problems today. The church is not functioning after the pattern that both Jesus Christ and the apostle Paul instituted. Paul's concern here is that every member has their particular function within the body of Christ and ministering to others with an attitude of superiority would hinder or destroy true sacrificial ministry and servant leadership.

Gilliland emphasizes this as a serious need within the body of Christ.

> When this spirit of responsibility, service, and trust is shared by all, and it is understood that God desires to be seen in the life of each new believer, both individual Christians and the whole church will be empowered for growth. Paul . . . does not permit inactivity, dependency on strong leaders, or preoccupation with being served to paralyze the convert. The Holy Spirit who convicts is also the Holy Spirit who gives the desire and power to serve. Each convert must be pressed into loving ministry at once and seek the special capacity God will give to serve (1998:143).

Church leadership must recognize and implement the fact that all spiritual gifts "are the work of one and the same Spirit, and he gives them to *each one*, just as he determines" (1 Cor. 12:11), "and the manifestation of the Spirit is given for the common good" (1 Cor. 12:7). Even though church leaders know this, is it really being put into practice? Are we really allowing the Holy Spirit the freedom to manifest Himself through all believers and not just a select few?

Women for too long have been discriminated against and not been able to take their rightful place within the body of Christ.

Paul demonstrated that spiritual gifts are endowments of power that enable us to carry out the vital functions of body life in Christ as members of His body. These endowments are a supernatural enablement so that supernatural results are produced.

In the New Testament, Jesus and the various New Testament writers placed the role of women in its proper biblical place. David L. Smith states, "Paul had more to say about women in the church than did any of the other New Testament writers" (1996:291). Women played a crucial role in the life of the Early Church, therefore, women must be allowed to function as God has gifted them to function in the church today.

The body of Christ today must recognize that God views women as His creation. How dare we consider them anything but equal in the body of Christ. There is today a lot of abuse of women in our society, whether, physical, emotional, psychological, and spiritual. How dare we treat God's creation with such disrespect! Jesus stated,

> "I have given them your word and the world has hated them, for they are not of the world any more than I am of the world. My prayer is not that you take them out of the world but that you protect them from the evil one. They are not of the world, even as I am not of it" (Jn. 17:14-16).

Peter likewise states,

> "Dear friends, I urge you, as aliens and strangers in the world, to abstain from sinful desires, which war against your soul" (1 Pet. 2:11).

When we place our faith in Jesus Christ, we become "aliens and strangers in the world" and as such we now conform to a higher standard of lifestyle. If, in our particular culture, disrespecting women whether physically, emotionally, psychologically, or spiritually is the norm, then since we are no longer of this world, we must allow the Holy Spirit to transform our behavior to that of our new heavenly culture. We must remember that in Jesus Christ we are all one and as we live in the unity of the Holy Spirit we will truly love one another.

> "A new command I give you: Love one another. As I have loved you, so you must love one another. By this all men will know that you are my disciples, if you love one another" (Jn. 13:34-35).

Chapter 5

Community Life in the
Early Church

The purpose of this chapter is to describe the household concept of ministry, community life and fellowship, the priesthood and ordination of all believers, and how each member of the Early Church sought to edify one another. It describes the community life within the Early Church and a necessary model and suggestions that the church today can implement into its life and ministry.

"After that, he poured water into a basin and began to wash his disciples' feet, drying them with the towel that was wrapped around him. . . . When he had finished washing their feet, he put on his clothes and returned to his place. 'Do you understand what I have done for you?' he asked them. 'You call me Teacher and Lord, and rightly so, for that is what I am. Now that I, your Lord and Teacher, have washed your feet, you also should wash one another's feet. I have set you an example that you should do as I have done for you. I tell you the truth, no servant is greater than his master, nor is a messenger greater than the one who sent him. Now that you know these things, you will be blessed if you do them'" (Jn. 13:5, 12-17).

The life and ministry of the Early Church was patterned after Jesus who gave us the greatest example of what it means to serve others through more than just words. He demonstrated servanthood by washing the disciple's feet (Jn. 13:12-17). In Scripture we find various references to Jesus being on His knees, however, the most precious is seen here when He washes His disciples feet. In Bible times it was only the lowest of all servants or slaves who would wash someone's feet, yet Jesus instructed them as leaders to set an example to "do as I have done for you" (Jn. 13:15). Leaders, in the body of Christ, should be the first to minister from a servant's position, which would bring healing and cleansing to the body of Christ, and would demonstrate true leadership.

Serving others was a critical part of being a disciple of Jesus that those who refuse, like Peter did initially, would not be considered a disciple. Jesus told Peter, "Unless I wash you, you have no part with me" (Jn. 13:8). Peter's response, "'Then, Lord,' Simon Peter replied, 'not just my feet but my hands and my head as well!'" (Jn. 13:9). Jesus washing Peter's feet showed that he was accepting the ministry, and servanthood of Jesus, and the necessity of cleansing his personality so that he would be fit to serve in the Kingdom of God. This external cleansing was a picture of spiritual cleansing from evil, therefore, Peter needed this cleansing in order to minister alongside Jesus. Jesus was teaching His disciples that in ministry (serving others), attitude and a servant's heart is important, however, more importantly, leaders are to set an example for others to follow. This is the example that the Early Church set in their life and ministry for others to follow and how the church today should also respond to other believers and non-believers. They were servants at heart patterned after the example of Jesus Christ.

House Churches in the Early Church

In Scripture we find various references to house churches. The first house church was located in the house of Lydia in Philippi (Acts 16:13-15). When Paul sent greetings to the Roman believers in Corinth he addressed "Gaius, my host and the host of the whole church" (Rom. 16:23). The city of Ephesus was the home of Priscilla and Aquila, two of Paul's closest companions in the ministry "who risked their own necks for my life" (Rom. 16:4), and also had a "church that meets at their house" (1 Cor. 16:19). Priscilla and Aquila after spending some time in Corinth and Ephesus now return to Rome and establish another "church that meets at their house" (Rom. 16:4-5). Philemon's home in Colosse was the gathering place for a house church "that meets in your home" (Phl. 2). However, there was another house church that met in Colosse at the house of "Nympha and the church in her house" (Col. 4:15).

New Testament Concept of Household

The apostle Paul used various metaphors to describe the church.[27] However, the metaphor of the household is one of the most important in the New Testament (Eph. 2:19-22; 1 Tim. 3:15). The basic unit in Greco-Roman society that influenced Paul's life and ministry was the concept of the household. The Greek word that used to describe the household was οἶκος *(oíkos)*, which referred to "a house, household, family, possessions; those who live within the house and their possessions" (Balz and Schneider 1990, 2:500).

The households at the time of Jesus and the Early Church were large, inclusive communities that consisted of the nuclear family, extended family, slaves, freedmen, servants, laborers, and at times business associates and tenants. The household was a hierarchical system where the owner of the house had full authority over everything and everyone within his household and also had obligations and was responsible for their well being. The atmosphere within the household was dependent upon economic, social, psychological, and religious factors. Membership within a house church created a sense of refuge, protection, security, and identity that could not be found in the

---

[27] *The body of Christ* (1 Cor. 12:27; Eph. 5:23-32), *the bride of Christ* (Mt. 25:6; 2 Cor. 11:2-3; Eph. 5:22-32), *the people of God* (Heb. 4:9; 1 Pet. 2:9-10), *the temple of God* (1 Cor. 3:16-17; Eph. 2:19-22; 1 Tim. 3:15), *the church of God* (Acts 20:28; 1 Cor. 1:2; 10:32; 11:16, 22; 15:9; 2 Cor. 1:1; 1 Th. 2:14; 2 Th. 1:4; 1 Tim. 3:5, 15), *the building of God* (1 Cor. 3:9; Eph. 2:20-22), *the flock of God* (Jn. 10; Acts 20:28; 1 Pet. 5:2), *the church of Christ* (Mt. 16:18; Rom. 16:16), *the people belonging to God* (1 Pet. 2:9), *the new man* (Eph. 2:14-15), *the congregations of the saints* (1 Cor. 14:33), *a royal priesthood* (1 Pet. 2:5, 9; Rev. 1:6; 5:10), *the church of the first-born* (Heb. 12:23).

political and social structures of society (Hawthorne and Martin 1993:417). Conversion within the house church was more than an individual decision, it was also seen as a decision based on the whole household. "Believe in the Lord Jesus, and you will be saved—you and your household" (Acts 16:31).

> In the ancient world, two types of traditional communities existed. These were the politeia, the public life of the city or state, and the oikonomia, the household order in which one was born or attached. These associations, however, did not provide participation for slaves, various dependents, the unmarried, and the outcasts, thereby creating disenchantment among many. Hence, increasing numbers of people began to find their desires fulfilled in a variety of voluntary associations which were multiplying, especially in Greek cultures. . . . The Pauline ideal encompassed all three of the contemporary human quests. First, the church was a voluntary association with a small group of like-minded people who regularly gathered together. In this way, it could fulfill the aspirations for a universal fraternity which educated Greeks, Romans, and Jews all contemplated upon. Second, the church had its roots in and thus took on the character of the household unit, a community for personal identity and intimacy for which people longed but seldom find. Finally, these small church groups were invested with a supranational and supratemporal significance, a common longing felt among the masses (Birkey 1988:37).

Development of the House Church

The house church was a natural outgrowth of the household concept that already existed. Paul always started with where the people were at spiritually and then built upon that leading them to Jesus Christ. He likewise did the same with the house church because he knew that it would be easier for them to follow something similar to their way of life. Barrett states,

> A house church is a group of people small enough to meet face-to-face, who have covenanted with God and each other to be the church under the authority of Christ and the guidance of the Spirit. A house church often meets in homes, although it may sometimes meet in public buildings. But more important than the place of

meeting is the closeness of relationships implied by the word "house" (1986:18).

Christianity emerged in the ancient world as a sect within Judaism, which gave the Early Church legal protection as it was being established. These small home-centered gatherings were an accepted pattern and each house church was allowed the freedom to move in the direction based on the needs of their community. This freedom positively affected the development of the Early Church (Birkey 1988:58).

The synagogue provided Paul with the means to proclaim the message of salvation that it is "by grace you have been saved, through faith" in Jesus Christ (Eph. 2:8). The Early Church imitated the worship service of the synagogue in Scripture reading and exposition, prayer and the common meal. Del Birkey states, "These small fellowships were not dependent on conforming to temple or synagogue worship, nor on buildings they had erected. Archaeological evidence suggests the average size household could accommodate about 30 to 35 comfortably" (1988:54). They also differed in that the Early Church practiced baptism and not circumcision, their worship included prophecy and speaking in tongues, women were allowed to minister, and there was no longer national or racial distinctions.

It may be presumed that some early converts to Christianity continued their membership in the local synagogue (Jas. 1:1). Being Jews as well as Christians, they may have blended into the life of the congregation or perhaps shared the building with the Jews. The antagonism of some Jews against the Christian converts (Acts 13:45; 14:2; 17:5-9) suggests, however, that this sort of arrangement could not have lasted long and the Christians would have been forced to meet in private homes and their own churches (Rom. 16:5; Acts 18:5-7; 20:20) (Matthews 1995:260).

This development of the house church affected the lives of the Early Church tremendously since the emphasis now was that of being a church family, the very household of God. Paul told the Ephesians, "Consequently, you are no longer foreigners and aliens, but fellow citizens with God's people and members of God's household, built on the foundation of the apostles and prophets, with Christ Jesus himself as the chief cornerstone" (2:19-20). Birkey states,

> Every home should be a church, for a church is where Jesus dwells. This goes far to explain why there is so much emphasis in the New Testament on family life and interpersonal relationships. The need for making faith work in daily homelife was surely intensified by the dynamic house church structure. We must not forget that the New Testament ideas of Christian education are based upon a 'Hebrew model' of the Old Testament, which placed the responsibility in the locus of homelife (cf. Deut. 6:1-9) (1988:55).

Community Life and Fellowship

The characteristics that distinguished this new community of believers from their society are many. The setting of this new community begins with Peter's sermon on the Day of Pentecost, which is the catalyst that forms this new community of believers. The original community, which consisted of 12 disciples in the gospels now grows to a congregation of 120 believers and then 3,000 more were added to their number on the Day of Pentecost. It appears that this community grew more in one day "about three thousand were added to their number that day" than the entire ministry of Jesus Christ. This coincides with Jesus telling His disciples that they "will do even greater things than these, because I am going to the Father" (Jn. 14:12). This was not referring to the *quality*, since no one would be able to supercede Jesus in this manner, but to the *quantity* of "greater things."

Luke in Acts 2:42-47 describes the ideal picture of the new community who were rejoicing in being worthy to receive the forgiveness of sins and the gift of the Holy Spirit (Acts 2:38) that had been poured out upon them. This new community of the Early Church "devoted themselves to the apostles' teaching." The Greek phrase προσκαρτεροῦντες τῇ δαχῇ τῶν ἀποστόλων means to "hold fast to, endure in, stand perpetually ready, persevere in, and emphasizes the persistence and submissive perseverance and tenaciousness of a self-enclosed group collectively oriented toward specific goals" (Balz and Schneider 1990, 3:172). The greater emphasis lies in the time element or duration, which is the key to persistence. This new community was constituted on the foundation of the apostolic teaching whose authority came from the Lord communicated through the apostles in the power and vitality of the Holy Spirit.

The Doctrines of the Early Church

"Therefore let us leave the elementary teachings about Christ and go on to maturity, not laying again the foundation of repentance from acts that lead to death, and of faith in God, instruction about baptisms, the laying on of hands, the resurrection of the dead, and eternal judgment" (Heb. 6:1-2).

What exactly did the apostles teach? Although, it appears that commentaries do not describe exactly what the apostles taught, they must have taught "the elementary teachings about Christ," which included His life and ministry. Once they have understood these "elementary teachings" they could then "go on to maturity." In Acts 2:42-47, Luke describes a young group of believers who had found a new life in Jesus Christ, which was constituted on the basis of the "apostles' teaching."

The apostles authority was based upon the teachings of Jesus Christ through the power of the Holy Spirit adhered to by the new community of believers. The apostles taught that the disciples and the new community of believers were to be "devoted" to two areas of belief's (teaching and fellowship) and two areas of practices (breaking of bread and prayer) in their life and ministry.

Teaching is the unveiling of God's New Testament economy concerning Christ and the church. Fellowship is the communion and communication between the believers in their communion and communication with God the Father and Christ the Son. Breaking of bread is the remembrance of the Lord in His accomplishment of God's full redemption. Prayer is cooperation with the Lord in heaven in carrying out of God's New Testament economy on earth (Lee 1985, 5:91).

The apostle's teaching is a complex subject and many authors of commentaries have not taken the time to expound on what they taught. The apostles' would have based their teachings largely upon the Nicene Creed[28] yet also included other doctrines, which are referenced in Hebrews 6:1-2. The Early Church studied and taught these doctrines because:

- It gave them substance to their newfound belief and confession of Jesus Christ.
- It brought stability to their lives in times of testing.
- It equipped them to "correctly handle the word of truth" (2 Tim. 2:15).
- It brought confidence to their new walk in Christ.
- It calmed their fears and cancelled their superstition.
- It gave them objective beliefs, which was the foundation to their Christian lives (Iverson and Asplund 1995:71).

Therefore, a short synopsis will aid in the understanding of what the Early Church might have believed.

---

[28] See Appendix D.

Table 8

The Apostles' Teaching
(Adapted from Iverson and Asplund 1995:70)

Salvation by Repentance and Faith	"Peter replied, 'Repent and be baptized, every one of you, in the name of Jesus Christ for the forgiveness of your sins. And you will receive the gift of the Holy Spirit' (Acts 2:38). "He then brought them out and asked, 'Sirs, what must I do to be saved?' They replied, 'Believe in the Lord Jesus, and you will be saved—you and your household'" (Acts 16:30-31).
Water Baptism by Immersion	"And he gave orders to stop the chariot. Then both Philip and the eunuch went down into the water and Philip baptized him. When they came up out of the water, the Spirit of the Lord suddenly took Philip away, and the eunuch did not see him again, but went on his way rejoicing" (Acts 8:38-39; 2:41).
The Baptism in The Holy Spirit	"While Peter was still speaking these words, the Holy Spirit came on all who heard the message. The circumcised believers who had come with Peter were astonished that the gift of the Holy Spirit had been poured out even on the Gentiles. For they heard them speaking in tongues and praising God" (Acts 10:44-46; Acts 2:38-39).
Laying on of hands and prophecy	"While they were worshiping the Lord and fasting, the Holy Spirit said, 'Set apart for me Barnabas and Saul for the work to which I have called them.' So after they had fasted and prayed, they placed their hands on them and sent them off" (Acts 13:2-3).
Resurrection of the Dead	"In Joppa there was a disciple named Tabitha (which, when translated, is Dorcas), who was always doing good and helping the poor. About that time she became sick and died, and her body was washed and placed in an upstairs room. Lydda was near Joppa; so when the disciples heard that Peter was in Lydda, they sent two men to him and urged him, 'Please come at once!' Peter went with them, and when he arrived he was taken upstairs to the room. All the widows stood around him, crying and showing him the robes and other clothing that Dorcas had made while she was still with them. Peter sent them all

	out of the room; then he got down on his knees and prayed. Turning toward the dead woman, he said, 'Tabitha, get up.' She opened her eyes, and seeing Peter she sat up" (Acts 9:36-40).
The Judgment of God	"Then Peter said, 'Ananias, how is it that Satan has so filled your heart that you have lied to the Holy Spirit and have kept for yourself some of the money you received for the land? Didn't it belong to you before it was sold? And after it was sold, wasn't the money at your disposal? What made you think of doing such a thing? You have not lied to men but to God.' When Ananias heard this, he fell down and died. And great fear seized all who heard what had happened. Then the young men came forward, wrapped up his body, and carried him out and buried him" (Acts 5:3-6). "You are a child of the devil and an enemy of everything that is right! You are full of all kinds of deceit and trickery. Will you never stop perverting the right ways of the Lord? Now the hand of the Lord is against you. You are going to be blind, and for a time you will be unable to see the light of the sun" (Acts 13:10-11).
The Lord's Supper	"For I received from the Lord what I also passed on to you: The Lord Jesus, on the night he was betrayed, took bread, and when he had given thanks, he broke it and said, 'This is my body, which is for you; do this in remembrance of me.' In the same way, after supper he took the cup, saying, 'This cup is the new covenant in my blood; do this, whenever you drink it, in remembrance of me.' For whenever you eat this bread and drink this cup, you proclaim the Lord's death until he comes" (1 Cor. 11:23-26).
False Doctrines	Both Jesus and Paul violently attacked false doctrines. Jesus condemned the scribes and Pharisees and called them "you hypocrites!" (Mt. 23:13, 15, 23, 25, 27); 'blind guides' (Mt. 23:16, 24); "blind fools" (Mt. 23:17); "whitewashed tombs" (Mt. 23:27); "You snakes! You brood of vipers!" (Mt. 23:33). Paul pronounced a cursed on anyone who preached another gospel (Gal. 1:8-9). He also called false teachers "dogs" and "mutilators of the flesh" (Phil. 3:2). Peter condemned false teachers who would bring "swift destruction on themselves" (2 Pet. 2:1; 3:12-14). The Epistle of Jude also attacks false teachers.

These new converts realized that man's search for absolute truth began with a relationship with God and His word. They discovered that they cannot base their beliefs on experience and interpretation and then search the Scripture to support their interpretation. They soon realized that their experience must be interpreted in light of the Word of God, which included every area of life such as: philosophy, psychology, theology, and religion (Iverson and Asplund 1995:64).

Even though the apostles taught sound, biblical doctrine they needed to be aware of those who would try to destroy what the Holy Spirit was accomplishing in the lives of these new converts. There were men who desired to hinder the work of the gospel through heresies, which was a serious threat to the spread of Christianity. Rolland Allen comments

> The great heresies in the early Church arose not from the rapid expansion resulting from the work of these unknown teachers; but in those churches which were longest established, and where the Christians were not so busily engaged in converting the heathen around them. The Church of that day was apparently quite fearless of any danger that the influx of large numbers of what we should call illiterate converts might lower the standard of church doctrine. She held the tradition handed down by the apostles, and expected the new converts to grow into it, to maintain it and to propagate it. And so in fact they did. The danger to the doctrine lay not in these illiterate converts on the outskirts; but at home, in places like Ephesus and Alexandria, amongst the more highly educated and philosophically minded Christians. It was against them that she had to maintain the doctrine (1960:48).

Therefore, teaching became a prominent feature of the Early Church to guard against the false teachings that were trying to confuse and destroy the work of the Holy Spirit. This was not only true among the Jewish believers (Acts 2:42; 4:2; 5:28, 42), but also the Gentile believers in Jerusalem. In each church that Paul and his coworkers established, systematic teaching was a vital ongoing process (Acts 15:35; 17:1-3, 10-13, 16f.; 18:1-11;

19:8-10). Even while Paul was in prison he continued his teaching ministry (Acts 28:23, 30-31) (Gilbrant 1986, 12:120).

They devoted themselves "to the fellowship," κοινωνία *(koinōnía)*, a common Greek term which "denotes, not the Christian society nor its community of goods, but the family fellowship established and expressed in the church's life" (Bromiley 1985:450). Brown adds, *"koinōnía* expresses something new and independent. It denotes the unanimity and unity brought about by the Spirit. The individual was completely upheld by the community" (1986, 1:642). It also assumes equality to the apostles' teaching, prompted by the Holy Spirit who creates unity within the Early Church.

> Paul regarded the entire Christian call to be a summons to "fellowship" with Jesus Christ. "Sharing" most notably takes place at the table of the Lord. For Paul, then, eating and drinking are more than mere symbols, though symbols are involved; eating and drinking at the Lord's table denote an inner "participation" with Christ. It is the ultimate expression of unity—the common bond— between Christ and His body the church (1 Cor. 10:16f.) (Gilbrant 1986, 13:367).

The term "fellowship" as used in Acts 2:42, indicates that to involve oneself in this fellowship meant the denial of personal interest and to join others in a common purpose. It meant devotion to the fellowship of the apostles in order to bring to fulfillment the divine purposes of God.

This new community was not another sect of Judaism, even though they continued their Jewish rituals and customs. They were a distinguished entity who proclaimed Jesus Christ as Lord and as Israel's Messiah, redeemer, and soon coming King. Smith states

> The fellowship of the primitive communities was not only spiritual, but also effected new and radical social changes. Gender, social, and economic gulfs were bridged. At the same time, Early Church fellowship was a quality of spiritual and interpersonal communion which transcended any mere social arrangement, yet which

engendered and was further enriched by novel social patterns
(1996:345).

This new community did not just affect certain areas of
society, it transformed every area, which should be logical since
the work of the Holy Spirit is a complete transformation, not
partial. However, as Michael Harper states, there is a paradox
of community.

> The quest for community will always fail, because community is
> not built by love of community, but by the love of the brethren.
> Koinonia is almost a by-product of the Spirit's activity as he
> produces that sort of love in our hearts. Those who love community
> more than people will destroy community, for people cannot
> successfully be used as a means (1 Jn. 3:14, 16) (1978:97).

Harper's statement here is powerful since it hits at the heart
of community life. The basis for community is the love shared
between our brothers and sisters in the Lord. This love is based
upon the Holy Spirit's administration of the God's love within
our hearts, which is then manifested outwardly towards others.

They devoted themselves "to the breaking of bread" or in
the Greek τῇ κλάσει τοῦ ἄρτου. This term is used only in Luke
24:35 and Acts 2:42, which refers to the sharing of a meal. The
"breaking of bread" or the Lord's Supper could not be observed
within the temple because, it was not a Jewish term for a meal,
so it had to be practiced within individual homes in connection
with a meal. The reference "They broke bread in their homes
and ate together" in 2:46 is to an actual meal (Barrett 1994,
1:165).

> Klasis is common in Greek literature for various kinds of breaking,
> including the fracture of bones, as well as the bending of knees. . . .
> It is apparent that the breaking of bread often refers to the opening
> action of a meal which the host would break a loaf of bread as
> indication that the meal was to begin. Later the phrase "breaking of
> bread" became a term for the Lord's Supper (Gilbrant 1986,
> 13:346).

When the disciples came together on the Day of Pentecost, the breaking of bread was a continuation of traditional fellowship, which had been established by Jesus and incorporated into the observance of the Lord's Supper. At first, the Lord's Supper was included with the common meal, however, it later became a separate aspect of the life of the community.

Finally, they devoted themselves "to prayer" or in the Greek ταῖς προσευχαῖς. Luke had earlier described the parallelism between the Holy Spirit's work as it related to Jesus and the Spirit's work in relation to the church. However, here in Acts, Luke now describes the parallelism between the prayer life of Jesus and the prayer life of the church. "The prayers," since the Greek here is in the plural, refers to formal prayers, which represented both Jews and Christians (Gaebelein 1981, 9:290).

Their focus was heavenward, toward the throne, on God Himself. Therefore, they gave themselves to a life of prayer. Jesus had earlier said "My house will be a house of prayer" (Lk. 19:46). This Early Church knew the necessity of seeking God and His will in prayer, and that a life of prayer involved a continual, daily devotion to prayer. A great church will be a praying church, because it depends upon God for its existence.

The reason for the power of prayer is that it engages God in the situation. The Early Church quickly learned to use prayer effectively because they began to be persecuted and saw the Lord's hand of protection upon their lives (Acts 8:1). Peter and John were rebuked by the Sanhedrin (Acts 4:1-22), when they returned to the assembly, prayer was the first order of the day (Acts 4:23-31). Later, when Peter was imprisoned, the church came together to pray (Acts 12:5). The Early Church was devoted to prayer as a way of life and God moved in their midst as a result (Acts 4:31).

The prayer life of this new community of believers followed the Jewish model, however the content of their prayers was focused upon Jesus and his life, teachings, and ministry. Prayer creates a bond between one another, it draws us together in a close, intimate relationship, which the Early Church understood. Prayer also resulted in a boldness to reach out to others with the same gospel of Jesus Christ that had transformed their lives. The Early Church believed

> That they had been called to a higher quality of life than could be expected of their society, and they took measures to safeguard it through their communities. . . . Early Christianity did not see themselves as isolated individuals; and the nature of those communities becomes clearer to us when we see them as household communities. It is striking how often the New Testament deals with issues in relation to the Christian community (Malherbe 1983:69).

This type of fellowship naturally resulted in an outward ministry *(diakonia)*, a sacrificial ministry of serving those in need. This type of service was best summed up by Jesus.

> "The Spirit of the Lord is on me, because he has anointed me to preach good news to the poor. He has sent me to proclaim freedom for the prisoners and recovery of sight for the blind, to release the oppressed, to proclaim the year of the Lord's favor" (Lk. 4:18-19).

He also told them "I tell you the truth, anyone who has faith in me will do what I have been doing. He will do even greater things than these, because I am going to the Father" (Jn. 14:12). Jesus taught His disciples that service is inherent in the gospel. These early Christians as a fellowship were concerned about showing compassion, justice, righteousness, and love for those in need. They demonstrated to others what they themselves had received.

> "Everyone was filled with awe, and many wonders and miraculous signs were done by the apostles. All the believers were together and had everything in common. Selling their possessions and goods, they gave to anyone as he had need. Every day they continued to meet together in the temple courts. They broke bread in their homes and ate together with glad and sincere hearts, praising God and enjoying the favor of all the people" (Acts 2:43-47a).

Evangelism in the Early Church

> "I am not ashamed of the gospel, because it is the power of God for
> the salvation of everyone who believes: first for the Jew, then for
> the Gentile. For in the gospel a righteousness from God is revealed,
> a righteousness that is by faith from first to last, just as it is written:
> 'The righteous will live by faith'" (Rom. 1:16-17).

The apostle Paul begins this Epistle to the Romans by
stating that both Jews and Gentiles are both guilty in the eyes of
God and are in need of being reconciled to God. Paul states that
both Jew (1:18-32) and Gentile (2:1-3:20) are in need of God's
righteousness, which is connected to the preaching of the
gospel. The promise of salvation was first given to Israel,
which Jesus states "I was sent only to the lost sheep of Israel"
(Mt. 15:24) and instructed His disciples to "Go rather to the lost
sheep of Israel" (Mt. 10:5-6).

Since the benefits of salvation can be appropriated by faith
through the propitiatory sacrifice of Jesus Christ, both Jews and
Gentiles have access to God (Eph. 2:11-22). However, Paul
now states that this salvation is "first for the Jew, then for the
Gentile." Paul in stating that salvation is "first for the Jew"
refutes Jewish exclusivism when he adds "then for the Gentile"
(Douglas 1962:1034). Paul, who was a Jew believed in a
Jewish Messiah, however, his purpose in life was to take the
gospel beyond the national and religious boundaries of Judaism
(Dunn 1988, 38a:40). John F. Walvoord and Roy B. Zuck give
a great summation of Romans 1:16-17,

> Because the Jews were God's Chosen People (11:1), the custodians
> of God's revelation (3:2), and the people through whom Christ
> came (9:5), they have a preference of privilege expressed
> historically in a chronological priority. As the Lord Jesus stated it,
> 'Salvation is from the Jews' (John 4:22). In Paul's ministry he
> sought out the Jews first in every new city (Acts 13:5, 14; 14:1;
> 17:2, 10, 17; 18:4, 19; 19:8). Three times he responded to their
> rejection of his message by turning to the Gentiles (Acts 13:46;
> 18:6; 28:25-28; cf. comments on Eph. 1:12) (1983:441).

It is interesting that Paul's primary focus was not evangelization of individuals and communities, but of the establishment of Christian communities. Jesus, likewise, focused primarily on making disciples more than proclaiming the good news of salvation. Jesus considered this a priority because

> Evangelism sprang from the community, and the community grew through its witness. Evangelism was not merely something that individual Christians did; rather it was the natural result of the presence and influence of the Christian community in the world. The community gave credibility to the verbal proclamation (Synder 1977:73).

This concept is vital for the church today if it is to be a force within our society. For the church to be an effective witness, our focus must be that of Jesus and Paul in developing Christian communities whose focus is a unified effort in the reaching the lost with the good news of Jesus Christ. We must get our priorities in the right order of building up one another and then reaching out to those outside of the community of Jesus Christ.

> If we compare our modern missionary work with the missionary work of the Early Church, this is what differentiates them: with us missions are the special work of a special organization; in the Early Church missions were not a special work, and there was no special organization. . . . The results are due, not to our organization, but to that undying spirit of love for the souls of men which Christ inspires. The modern organization is only the form in which we have expressed that spirit; and a time may come when organization, which seems to us to be absolutely necessary, may cease to be necessary, or may take such different shape as to be hardly recognizable; for it has within it elements of weakness which betray its temporary character (Allen 1960:96).

The rapid expansion of the Early Church was due to the spontaneous activity of its members. The gospel had produced within each of them a natural instinctive desire to witness to others, a contagious joy unspeakable. Each person had been led to Christ by the spontaneous zeal of those who had already experienced His salvation.

> The spontaneous expansion of the Church reduced to its elements is a very simple thing. It asks for no elaborate organization, no large finances, and great numbers of paid missionaries. In its beginning it may be the work of one man, and that a man neither learned in the things of this world, nor rich in the wealth of this world. The organization of a little church on the apostolic model is also extremely simple, and the most illiterate converts can use it, and the poorest are sufficiently wealthy to maintain it.
>
> No one, then, who feels within himself the call of Christ to embark on such a path as this need say, I am too ignorant, I am too inexperienced, I have too little influence, or I have not sufficient resources. The first apostles of Christ were in the eyes of the world "unlearned and ignorant" men: it was not until the Church had endured a persecution and had grown largely in numbers that Christ called a learned man to be His apostle (Allen 1960:156).

Church Growth in the Early Church

> "Praising God and enjoying the favor of all the people. And the Lord added to their number daily those who were being saved" (Acts 2:47).

Billy Graham said,

> The early church had no Bibles, no seminaries, no printing presses, no literature, no educational institutions, no radio, no television, no automobiles, no airplanes; and yet within one generation the gospel had been spread to most of the known world. The secret of the spread of this gospel was the power of the Holy Spirit.
>
> Today in the face of vastly improved methods of communication the power of the Holy Spirit is being neglected. We are trying to do things in our own strength, and as a result we are failing (1953:182).

The theme of church growth is a primary emphasis and is described throughout the Book of Acts, and is seen in the words "added"[29] (Acts 2:41, 47; 5:14; 11:24; 12:3; 13:36); "turned" (Acts 3:19; 9:35, 40; 11:21; 14:15, 19, 21, 36; 16:18; 26:18, 20; 8:27);[30] "grew" (Acts 4:4); "to increase" (Acts 6:1, 7; 7:17; 9:31; 12:24); "to grow" (Acts 6:7; 7:17; 12:24; 19:20).[31]

In each of these instances church growth was the result. The gospel is clearly presented in Acts as "the power of God for salvation to everyone who believes" (Rom. 1:16). It is able to overcome linguistic differences between Christians, it can conquer idolatry, and successfully face opposition. Luke emphatically stressed the fact of church growth in his account of the development of the Early Church.

There are many other examples of church growth in the Book of Acts such as: Philip and the Ethiopian eunuch (Acts 8:26-40); the conversion of Lydia and her household (Acts 16:11-15); the salvation of the jailer and his household when Paul and Silas were in prison (Acts 16:29-34); in Berea "Many of the Jews believed, as did also a number of prominent Greek women and many Greek men" (Acts 17:12); Paul's sermon at

---

[29] "The lexical form of προστίθημι (prostíthēmi) used here means 'to place near, add to, increase, continue, do again, repeat, give, grant, to proceed' and referred to men and women being added to or included into a society (Gilbrant 1986, 15:348). Bromiley states that in secular Greek this means 'to put to,' 'to add to,' 'to shut,' middle 'to attach oneself to,' 'to win,' 'to join' (cf. also 'to win over')" (1985:1181).

[30] "The lexical form of ἐπέστρεψω (epistréphō) also ὑποστρέφω (hypostrepho) are used in (Acts 14:21) and means "to turn, turn back, return" (Gilbrant 1986, 12:562). Bromiley states that it refers to "turning aside, turning back, restoring, and to convert to" and "to believe and to be converted go together" (1985:1096).

[31] "The lexical form of γίνομαι (gínomai), has various references in Acts and means 'to be, to come into being, to be made, be done, to happen, to become, to be celebrated'" (Gilbrant 1986, 11:613). Acts also uses the lexical form of πληθύνω (plēthýnō), which refers 'to be increased, multiply, grow, spread' (Gilbrant 1986, 15:209); and αὐξάνω (auxánō), which describes 'to make to grow, increase, become greater'" (Gilbrant 1986, 11:489).

Athens "A few men became followers of Paul and believed" (Acts 17:34);

"Crispus, the synagogue ruler, and his entire household believed in the Lord; and many of the Corinthians who heard him believed and were baptized" (Acts 18:8). However, before Paul's conversion on the road to Damascus, he "began to destroy the church. Going from house to house, he dragged off men and women and put them in prison. Those who had been scattered preached the word wherever they went" (Acts 8:3-4). They "never stopped teaching and proclaiming the good news that Jesus is the Christ" (Acts 5:42).

Three Types of Church Growth

Luke, in the Book of Acts, describes at least three kinds of church growth: numerical, geographical, and spiritual. The first is numerical growth, which Acts strongly emphasizes. However, Luke did not worship numbers, he certainly did not ignore them either! Numerical growth refers to the eleven remaining apostles and described the believers in the first prayer meeting as numbering 120 (Acts 1:13-15).

After Pentecost, those who accepted the message were baptized, which numbered about 3,000 (2:41). Their influence spread through entire families, villages, and towns and many were added to their numbers (16:11-34). In this way the Christian message reached people who shared a common background, culture, or geography. Even though there must have been biological growth within the Early Church, the Book of Acts main focus is that of conversion growth, for the church was just beginning its work in the world and therefore could not rely on the other forms of growth at all.

The second is geographical growth, because the gospel spread not only from one individual to another, but also from place to place. This development is clearly seen in Acts, since the gospel spread from Jerusalem to Rome (Acts 1:8; 9:15). The gospel was not restricted to Jerusalem, because its message was heard in Lydda, Sharon, and Joppa (9:35, 42); Samaria (8:5, 12), and then into Phoenicia, Cyprus, and Antioch (11:19-26). The gospel spread gradually from its Jewish matrix to include the known world. As Peter declared to the household of Cornelius, "I now realize how true it is that God does not show favoritism but accepts men from every nation who fear him and do what is right" (Acts 10:34-35).

The geographical expansion of the gospel was supported by the strong conviction that the gospel is for every person. "I am not ashamed of the gospel, because it is the power of God for the salvation of everyone who believes: first for the Jew, then for the Gentile" (Rom. 1:16). Peter, likewise in reminding his readers concerning the day of the Lord that God does "not want anyone to perish, but everyone to come to repentance" (2 Pet. 3:9).

The third is spiritual growth, which in the Early Church was not only quantitative growth, but qualitative. Even though there was a rapid increase in numbers and in geographical outreach, there was definite growth in spiritual life as the Christian communities developed throughout the Mediterranean and the Roman Empire. The gospel as it spread brought an increase in godly living. Luke throughout the Book of Acts uses the motif of fear[32] to create a sense of awe in those who received the gospel and those who were influenced by the gospel. A great example of this fear is when Luke speaks of the church's activity in Judea, Galilee, and Samaria (Acts 9:31), which refers to the numerical growth and spiritual encouragement of the

---

[32] "Luke uses the Greek word φόβος *(phóbos)* (2:43; 5:5, 11; 9:31; 19:17), which means 'to fear, terror, reverence, respect, awe.' 'But the glory of the gospel is that a new relationship with God overwhelms these negative aspects of fear, delivers believers from bondage, and gives them a spirit of adoption (son-placing) so that they confidently call God 'Father.' It is a relationship of love and trust. 'Fear' *(phóbos)* is no longer a fear of judgment for the believer. In addition, reverence towards God is always coupled with love for Him; this love, then will cast out all 'fear' (1 Jn. 4:18)" (Gilbrant 1986, 16:446).

Holy Spirit resulting from a lifestyle of "living in the fear of the Lord."

The martyrdom of Stephen (7:59), the faithful manner in which Philip preached (8:4-40), and the courage of the early Christians in facing persecution (5:27-33, 40-42; 16:19-25) all bear witness to their growth in grace. Indeed the leaders of the church gave attention to this nurturing process, "strengthening the disciples and encouraging them to remain true to the faith. 'We must go through many hardships to enter the kingdom of God'" (14:22; cf. 15:32, 35, 41; 18:23).

Overall, Luke presents a balanced picture of church growth that included numerical, geographical, and spiritual growth. To Luke, the Christian faith was truly an evangelistic faith, in which believers are to reach out to others and draw them to Jesus Christ. The Christian faith is also a missionary faith, which crossed national and cultural barriers to bring the gospel to every individual. Finally, the Christian faith is concerned with the edification and spiritual development of all of God's people. Luke's symmetrical picture of the Early Church gives careful attention to each of these factors.

Characteristics of Early Church Growth

There are seven characteristics of the Early Church that aided in its rapid growth. The first is that it was a witnessing church. These early Christians shared their faith in Jesus Christ with boldness (Acts 4:13, 29-31). Just before Jesus' ascension, He instructed His apostles "Do not leave Jerusalem, but wait for the gift my Father promised, which you have heard me speak about. For John baptized with water, but in a few days you will be baptized with the Holy Spirit" (Acts 1:4-5).

While "the apostles continued to testify to the resurrection of the Lord Jesus" (4:33), Stephen, Philip, Apollos, Aquila, and Priscilla, likewise worked together with them. It was an united effort as everyone helped and encouraged each other in the task of reaching out for Christ. Ordinary men and women planted churches in such places as Damascus, Phoenicia, Cyprus, Antioch, and Rome (9:10; 11:19; 28:13-14). There was no important people or mission boards to initiate a new work; they simply saw a need and did whatever was necessary to fulfill it.

After "a great persecution broke out against the church at Jerusalem, and all except the apostles were scattered throughout Judea and Samaria" (Acts 8:1) "Those who had been scattered preached the word wherever they went" (8:4). The early Christians had a compulsive, eager desire to bear witness to Christ. The apostles declared "We are witnesses of these things, and so is the Holy Spirit, whom God has given to those who obey him" (5:32; cf. v. 42). While the apostles had a unique role as the original eyewitnesses of Christ (1:21-22), every believer without exception was expected to share his or her faith in Christ with others. These ordinary church members were active partners in the Christian mission. They included John Mark's mother (12:12), Lydia the businesswoman from Thyatira (16:14), Gaius, and Aristarchus (19:29), and other traveling companions of Paul (20:4).

Second, it was a praying church. Prayer was a central focus of each of the Christian communities (Acts 2:42; cf. 3:1). The prayer life of this new community had begun from a prayer meeting in an upper room in Jerusalem, when 120 faithful people looked to God for the promised outpouring of the Holy Spirit (1:12-15; cf. 2:1-4). The importance of prayer was seen in the role of the leaders of the church, who pledged to give their attention "to prayer, and to the ministry of the Word" (6:4). The church faced each crisis on its knees in earnest prayer (1:24; 4:24-31; 12:5). The power of prayer can be seen in the experience of Paul and Silas at Philippi. Imprisoned, stripped, and beaten, these two men at midnight were "were praying and singing hymns to God" (16:25).

Third, it was a united church. There was an incredible bond of unity that existed in the Early Church. These believers understood what it meant "for brothers to dwell together in unity!" (Ps. 133:1). Luke describes this unity as ὁμοῦ *(homou)* or ὁμοθυμαδόν, *(homothumadón)* "with one mind, by common consent, together, with one accord" (Gilbrant 1986, 14:345). He also describes the believers as being united in worship (Acts 2:46; 5:12), in prayer (2:42; 4:24), and in decision-making (15:25). Luke stressed the fact that the believers came together frequently, both in church life (2:42-47; 4:32-37; 5:12-16) and ἐπὶ τὸ αὐτό (1:15; 2:1, 44; cf. Lk. 17:35), suggests being in church fellowship.

Fourth, it was a Spirit-filled church. In Acts 1:4, 8, Jesus had promised His disciples that the Holy Spirit would empower them as His witnesses. The key to the effectiveness of the witness of the Early Church was due to the inflow of the Spirit into their lives. The Holy Spirit created within the hearts of Peter and John such boldness that when they "realized that they were unschooled, ordinary men, they were astonished and they took note that these men had been with Jesus" (Acts 4:13). This same boldness (παρρησία)[33] was also characteristic of the other leaders such as Stephen, Philip, and Apollos.

There are many references to the guidance of the Holy Spirit in the lives of the saints. The Council at Jerusalem under the guidance of the Holy Spirit sent a letter to Gentile believers with the introduction, "It seemed good to the Holy Spirit and to us" (Acts 15:28). On another occasion "After they prayed, the place where they were meeting was shaken. And they were all filled with the Holy Spirit and spoke the word of God boldly" (Acts 4:31). The Holy Spirit, while the church at Antioch was "worshiping the Lord and fasting," directed them to "Set apart for Me Barnabas and Saul for the work to which I have called them" (Acts 13:2). Philip in speaking with the Ethiopian eunuch was conscious of the Holy Spirit's guidance told him to "Go to that chariot and stay near it" (Acts 8:29; cf. Ananias in

---

[33] "The Book of Acts shows that *parrhēsía* was a primary characteristic of early apostolic preaching and testifying. They 'boldly, fearlessly' and 'frankly' proclaimed the good news. They concealed nothing (e.g., Acts 2:22-24); they did not fear the consequences of their proclamation (Acts 4:13, 29, 31)" (Gilbrant 1986, 15:103).

9:15). Paul's ministry from the very beginning of his Christian life demonstrated that he was a person "filled with the Holy Spirit" (Acts 9:17).

Fifth, it was a Christ-centered church. This Early Church's primary focus was on the person and work of Jesus of Nazareth. The Early Church proclaimed that "God anointed Jesus of Nazareth with the Holy Spirit and power, and how he went around doing good and healing all who were under the power of the devil, because God was with him" (Acts 10:38). Their witness was to the unique place of Jesus Christ as the one and only Savior of the lost world, "Salvation is found in no one else, for there is no other name under heaven given to men by which we must be saved" (Acts 4:12).

Jesus Christ was the heart and soul of the life of the church, and the church grew as the Lord Jesus was lifted up. "But I, when I am lifted up from the earth, will draw all men to myself" (Jn. 12:32). Through Jesus a new way of access had been opened for men and women to enjoy fellowship with the living God. At the very center of this early community was an emphasis not only on repentance toward God but also faith in the Lord Jesus Christ (Acts 2:38; cf. Lk. 24:47; Acts 16:31). The Christocentric character of church life is indicated in the speeches of the early Christian leaders (e.g., Peter, 2:22-24; 3:6, 16; 10:36-38; Philip, 8:5, 35; Stephen, 7:56, 59). This is also strongly suggested by the warm, loving, unselfish lifestyle of the early Christian community to which reference has already been made (Acts 2:42-47).

Sixth it was a sacrificial church. The growth of the Early Church was the direct result of being persecuted for their faith (Acts 4:3; 5:18; 12:1-4). Stephen encountered the same hostility (Acts 7:54-60). Luke knew that persecution served to purify the church and must be handled with patience and perseverance.

> "But before all this, they will lay hands on you and persecute you.
> They will deliver you to synagogues and prisons, and you will be

brought before kings and governors, and all on account of my name. This will result in your being witnesses to them. But make up your mind not to worry beforehand how you will defend yourselves. For I will give you words and wisdom that none of your adversaries will be able to resist or contradict. You will be betrayed even by parents, brothers, relatives and friends, and they will put some of you to death. All men will hate you because of me. But not a hair of your head will perish. By standing firm you will gain life" (Lk. 21:12-19).

Jesus taught His disciples to expect hard times, opposition, and persecution and Acts contains many encounters with hostile forces. Stephen and James were martyred (Acts 7:54-60; 12:2), the apostles frequently arrested (Acts 4:1-4; 16:16-40), and the early disciples were scattered after persecution broke out against the church in Jerusalem (Acts 8:1). Barnabas and Paul, "risked their lives for the name of our Lord Jesus Christ" (Acts 15:26). This sacrificial spirit has been seen throughout church history, but nothing like that of the Early Church.

Lastly, it was a compassionate church. This compassionate attitude of the Early Church shines throughout the Book of Acts. This was demonstrated in the way that they shared their possessions with each other:

"All the believers were one in heart and mind. No one claimed that any of his possessions was his own, but they shared everything they had. With great power the apostles continued to testify to the resurrection of the Lord Jesus, and much grace was upon them all. There were no needy persons among them. For from time to time those who owned lands or houses sold them, brought the money from the sales and put it at the apostles' feet, and it was distributed to anyone as he had need" (Acts 4:32-35).

This sharing was voluntary, temporary, and spontaneous, but it speaks volumes of the kind of loving, compassionate people who were apart of this Christian fellowship. Evangelism and social action was a united force that influenced society. This fellowship of believers not only preached the gospel, they ministered to the practical needs of their members (6:1-7) and reached out in generous, loving service to help and heal outsiders as well (e.g., the healing of the father of Publius by Paul, 28:7-10). They were a fellowship who sincerely loved one another. They viewed their integrity and credibility in such high regards that they treated the hypocrisy of Ananias and Sapphira (Acts 5:1-11) severely, because it threatened the life of the community.

Community Life and the Priesthood of All Believers

"But you are a chosen people, a royal priesthood, a Holy nation, a people belonging to God, that you may declare the praises of him who called you out of darkness into his wonderful light. Once you were not a people, but now you are the people of God; once you had not received mercy, but now you have received mercy" (1 Pet. 2:9-10).

The apostle Peter addresses the exiles of the Dispersion,

"To God's elect, strangers in the world, scattered throughout Pontus, Galatia, Cappadocia, Asia and Bithynia, who have been chosen according to the foreknowledge of God the Father, through the sanctifying work of the Spirit, for obedience to Jesus Christ and sprinkling by his blood" (1 Pet. 1:1-2).

These scattered Christians composed of both Jews and Gentiles are the priesthood and the people of God. This priesthood is no longer based on racial or national lines, but on belonging to the community of Christ. Peter describes them as "Once you were not a people, but now you are the people of God" (1 Pet. 2:10). Peter assures them that wherever they are and whoever they are, these new believers corporately are the people of God. Peter draws from Exodus 19:5-6 and Isaiah 43:20-21 as he describes the church as a corporate unity of people, "a chosen people, a royal priesthood, a holy nation" (1 Pet. 2:9), rather than describing the priesthood as being individualistic. The term "chosen people" joins the believers to Christ, while "royal priesthood" places them all within the priesthood and that they belong to the King of Kings, Jesus Christ.

New Testament Priesthood of All Believers[34]

It is interesting that the term "priest" is not used in the New Testament of a minister or order within the church. Jesus also does not use images of the priestly ministry, but He does refer to secular society. He never uses the title to describe Himself or His disciples as priests. The word "priest" is often used in relation to the Jews, their priests and high priests—but never in regard to the Christian believer.

Jesus, like the priests of the Old Testament, is appointed by God (Heb. 5:4-6). Jesus does not inherit the established idea of the priesthood because He is a descendent from the tribe of Judah, not from the tribe of Levi. It is not traditional since He is from "the order of Melchizedek, not in the order of Aaron" (Heb. 7:11) (Küng 1971:364). The priesthood that Jesus established is a permanent priesthood "because Jesus lives forever" (Heb. 7:24).

Jesus has come as the "great high priest" (Heb. 4:14) and offered Himself as the ultimate and supreme sacrifice, there is no longer any need to offer up physical sacrifices. He has made all believers a part of the priesthood and able to offer up "spiritual sacrifices acceptable to God through Jesus Christ (1 Pet. 2:4-5). In this new order of the priesthood, all believers are not only the stones that form this "spiritual house," we are the priesthood that serves in it. These "spiritual sacrifices" refer to the praise and thanksgiving "the fruit of lips that confess his name," but also doing good and sharing with others are sacrifices that please God (Heb. 13:15-16). These "spiritual sacrifices" also refer to living a life of holiness, which does not include rituals, but a life that daily renounces one's sins and being committed to a life of divine obedience (Rom. 12:1).

---

[34] For a discussion on Old Testament Priesthood see Appendix C.

This new access to God, the institution of the priesthood of all believers, would not have occurred if Jesus had not have been crucified, died, buried and resurrected from the dead. It was at the moment that "he gave up his Spirit" (Mt. 27:50), which He did willingly, that access to God was completed, opening forever the door to a personal relationship with Jesus Christ and the institution of the priesthood of all believers.

> "The reason my Father loves me is that I lay down my life—only to take it up again. No one takes it from me, but I lay it down of my own accord. I have authority to lay it down and authority to take it up again. This command I received from my Father" (Jn. 10:17-18).

It was at Jesus' death, that "the curtain of the temple was torn in two from top to bottom. The earth shook and the rocks split. The tombs broke open and the bodies of many Holy people who had died were raised to life" (Mt. 27:51-52). The veil that was torn in two, which had excluded the people from the Shekinah presence of God, signified that all those who believe in Jesus Christ have full access to the presence of God. This earthquake that shook and split the rocks, also occurred at the giving of the law on Mount Sinai "the whole mountain trembled violently" (Ex. 19:18; Ps. 18:7), and was prophesied by Haggai (2:6-7, 21) (Simeon 1956, 17:602).

Jesus' life, death and resurrection, also brought a change in the priesthood and a change in the law as the writer to the Hebrews explains "For when there is a change of the priesthood, there must also be a change of the law" (Heb. 7:12). As Jesus stated earlier "Do not think that I have come to abolish the Law or the Prophets; I have not come to abolish them but to fulfill them" (Mt. 5:17).

The New Testament priesthood was not based on the human mediatory hierarchy as in the Old Testament. Jesus opened the way so that all believers can have the privilege and responsibility to function as priests. This means that all believers can participate in the fulfillment of the church's mandate by using their God-given abilities and spiritual giftedness to edify the whole community. "Now to each one the manifestation of the Spirit is given for the common good" (1 Cor. 12:7), "Each one should use whatever gift he has received to serve others, faithfully administering God's grace in its various forms" (1 Pet. 4:10).

> We see this principle operative in the Early Church. Crucial decisions pertaining to ministry—such as the choosing of Judas' replacement (Acts 1:23-26), the selection of the first deacons (Acts 6:3-6), and the commissioning of Paul and Barnabas (Acts 13:3)— were made by an entire congregation. Even the Jerusalem Council did not involve merely a select few, but the entire congregation (15:22). And the Early writers addressed their epistles to entire churches, thereby reinforcing the importance of the people as a whole in the life and decision-making of the local congregations.
>
> This does not deny the crucial role of leaders, however. Our life together is best facilitated when leaders equip the whole people for their task (Eph. 4:11-13). By teaching and through personal example, leaders ought to assist each Church member in becoming an active, informed, conscientious participant, who shoulders the responsibilities of membership and seeks the Spirit's leading (Grenz 1996:244).

Ordination of All Believers

> Ordination is that act whereby the Church sets apart persons whom the sovereign Spirit has selected and endowed for the fulfillment of special leadership tasks in service to the people of God. Therefore, ordination is a confirmation that the Spirit has called, gifted, and empowered a person for pastoral ministry (1 Tim. 4:14; 2 Tim. 1:6-7). Ordination also marks a public commissioning of someone whom the Spirit has called (Acts 13:3; cf. Num. 27:18-23) (Grenz 1996:248).

Ordination is more than the setting apart someone for a pastoral ministry, it involves setting apart everyone who has been called by the Holy Spirit to fulfill a specific ministry. Therefore, this includes all members of the body of Christ and not just a select few as in the Old Testament pattern of the priesthood. The dichotomy between the priest and laity

> Is one of the principle obstacles to the Church effectively being God's agent of the Kingdom today because it creates the false idea that only "Holy men," namely, ordained ministers, are really qualified and responsible for leadership and significant ministry. In the New Testament there are functional distinctions between various kinds of ministries but no hierarchical division between priest and laity (Synder 1977:95).

We must always remember that the New Testament never describes two classes of Christians—"ministers" and "laity"— as we find in churches today. We are all ministers of the gospel of Jesus Christ and as ministers are appointed for specific roles within the church. We must remember that by focusing only on the individual, the needs of the church are often forgotten or neglected.

> In appointing ministers for a congregation, it is as important to consider the needs of the church as it is to consider the character and the education of the individual; but by looking solely at the individual we forget the church. In the early Church we find local men ordained for the local church. They were ordained for that church; and they did not seek for some congenial sphere wherever they might see an opening or could obtain preferment. Thus the link between the church and the ministry was maintained. But in our system, when the minister is considered a purely personal gift, men seek for themselves, or are sent by authority, to occupy this post or that, without any regard to the link which is thus snapped, and the consequence is that they often look upon "churches" simply as places which offer them opportunities for the exercise of their gifts, or as steps in a ladder of preferment. But the link thus broken is not as unimportant one. . . . Where the whole population moves from place to place with extreme ease and readiness, the evil is not so apparent; but in a country where generation after generation lives in the ancestral village, the link between the local church and its ministers is of great importance, and the importance of a stranger to act as minister to people whom he does not know intimately, and who does not know him and his whole family intimately, is a serious evil (Allen 1960:130).

The practice of setting apart people for ministry has been central pattern of church life throughout the Christian era. Both Old and New Testaments selected leaders. In the Old Testament, the act of laying on of hands was practiced in the process of ordination and signified the investing of leadership responsibility and authority. The Lord instructed Moses to lay his hands upon Joshua in the presence of "Eleazar the priest and the entire assembly and commission him" (Num. 27:18-23). Another act of ordination was the anointing with oil, which symbolized the setting apart of a person for leadership. Three primary offices are associated with the anointing of oil—prophet, priest, and king.

Jesus used the concept of ordination when He appointed the twelve disciples to follow Him in His mission, "that they might be with him and that he might send them out to preach" (Mk. 3:13-14). He later appointed seventy others "and sent them two by two ahead of him to every town and place where he was about to go" (Lk. 10:1). The Jerusalem church commissioned seven men through the laying on of hands (Acts 6:6), and later Paul and Barnabas were appointed this same way by the church in Antioch (Acts 13:1-3). Grenz concludes this topic by stating,

> Because it is grounded in the life of the community, ordination to pastoral ministry arises out of the priesthood of all believers. All members share the ministry of the community. To this end, all are called and ordained by the Holy Spirit to ministry. Baptism is the sign of our universal ordination, for this act signifies our new birth by the Spirit, our new identity as disciples of Jesus, and our new relationship to one another as participants in the one fellowship of Christ. Ordination to pastoral ministry, therefore, is embedded in the Spirit's universal calling of all to the ministry of the Church and his universal endowment of all for this task (1994:737).

Ordination does not elevate one person above another, however, it does commission a person to fulfill a leadership role in order that the entire priesthood of believers is edified.

Community Life and Ministry

"Each one should use whatever gift he has received to serve others, faithfully administering God's grace in its various forms. If anyone speaks, he should do it as one speaking the very words of God. If anyone serves, he should do it with the strength God provides, so that in all things God may be praised through Jesus Christ. To him be the glory and the power for ever and ever. Amen" (1 Pet. 4:10-11).

The purpose of the gifts of the Holy Spirit is, first of all, that God will be glorified and second, is the edification of all believers. It is only as we edify one another that God is glorified. Also, it is only as we edify one another that we are edified. Karl Barth makes it clear regarding individual edification; "no such thing is ever envisaged in the New Testament. The New Testament speaks always of the upbuilding of the community. I can edify myself only as I edify the community" (IV, 1958, 2:627).

However the Holy Spirit chooses to manifest Himself, His purpose is always edification, the building up, of the body of Christ. The Lord desires that His people become mature, strengthened as a community, which is achieved, only as we edify one another. Therefore, the manifestation of any gift of the Holy Spirit that does not result in the edification of the body of believers is inappropriate and out of order. Through this mutual edification, God's power is seen, not human goodness or natural ability, which results in God being glorified through His creation.

The idea is that in every incident of ministry by Christians God's glory or reputation will be enhanced or revealed. It may be simply a sense that one is in the presence of God's merciful and gracious character (e.g., Luke 18:43; Acts 4:21) or that God's character shows in the life of those with whom he is identified (e.g., 1 Cor. 6:20). In whatever way by whatever gift the goal of ministry is to bring glory (i.e., honor) to God (cf. 1:3) (Davids 1990:162).

Peter divides all spiritual gifts into two categories: verbal communication and practical service. Peter states, "If anyone speaks, he should do it as one speaking the very words of God," which includes all the speaking gifts[35] for the edification of others. The reference here is not only pastors, elders, or other church leaders, but for all believers to allow the Holy Spirit to exercise these gifts through them for the edification of the body of Christ. This speaking is not for the edification of one's self, but is to be spoken "as one speaking the very words of God." He also states, "If anyone serves, he should do it with

The New Testament speaks always of the upbuilding of the community. I can edify myself only as I edify the community.

the strength God provides," which includes all the serving gifts[36] for the edification of others. These gifts are not something outside a person's control, but abilities given by the Holy Spirit that the individual must grow in and practice daily. Therefore, the Christian is to be a steward[37] of the gift(s). Peter views the Christian believer as a steward over the gift(s) that have been given by the Holy Spirit. Unless these gift(s) are based on "the strength God provides" the steward's ministry will be ineffective. God only gives us strength to accomplish His purposes.

---

[35] The speaking gifts include: faith, prophecy, teaching, evangelism, preaching, a message of wisdom, and knowledge, tongues and its interpretation. (See Rom. 12:6-8; 1 Cor. 12:8-10, 28-30; 13:1-2; Eph. 4:11).

[36] The serving gifts include: gifts of healing, workers of miracles, wisdom, knowledge, faith, discerning of spirits, apostles, prophets, evangelists, pastors and teachers, exhortation, serving, distributing to the needs of others, leadership, mercy, administration. (See Rom. 12:6-8; 1 Cor. 12:8-10, 28-30; 13:1-2; Eph. 4:11).

[37] "The steward was the person in a household (often a slave) who was responsible for managing the householder's business and property, including providing what was needed for the family members, slaves, and hired laborers" (Davids 1990:160).

The Holy Spirit is the giver of the gifts "and he gives them to each one, just as he determines" (1 Cor. 12:11). Since this is true, then, we can say that each Christian has the ability to be used by God in all the gifts. The Holy Spirit living within them can and will manifest the gift(s) that will meet the needs of the moment. If the gift of healing is needed for a particular situation then He will give that gift to the person when it is needed. The Holy Spirit can operate each of the gifts at different times, through the same person as they are needed; though some gifts will be stronger than others.

Mutual Edification

"For the kingdom of God is not a matter of eating and drinking, but of righteousness, peace and joy in the Holy Spirit, because anyone who serves Christ in this way is pleasing to God and approved by men. Let us therefore make every effort to do what leads to peace and to mutual edification" (Rom. 14:14-19).

The Greek phrase τῆς οἰκοδομῆς τῆς εἰς ἀλλήλους (mutual edification) is used literally and means, the building up *into* one another, or mutual edification. Paul here is referring to a process of building up, figuratively of spiritual strengthening of the body of Christ as a whole more than the individual edification of believers.

Paul is referring to two parties who have been guilty of judging one another. He encourages them to pursue peace, which provides the atmosphere for mutual edification to occur. Edification was the key word that Paul used in addressing the problems created by the manifestation of spiritual gifts in the church at Corinth (1 Cor. 14:5, 12, 26).

Mutual edification implies that the strong, despite their tendency to look down on the weak, may actually learn something from them. It may be that they will come to appreciate loyalty to a tender conscience and begin to search their own hearts to discover that they have cared more about maintaining their position than about loving their weaker brethren. Through the fresh manifestation of

love by the strong the weak will be lifted in Spirit and renewed in
faith and life (Gaebelein 1976, 10:149).

Paul is warning them that through judging one another they are
actually destroying the "work of God" and that restoring them
to a functioning instrument of divine purpose will involve a lot
of time and labor.

Edification is frequently used in the New Testament in a
metaphorical sense of the building up in character, of a church
(Mt. 16:18), or of an individual as in Paul's epistles (2 Cor.
10:8; 13:10; Eph. 4:12, 16). Jesus taught His disciples mutual
edification when He washed their feet and instructed them to do
likewise (Jn. 12:12-17). The Christian life is not an individual
attempt to strive for perfection; it is a community effort,
attainable only through reciprocal edification.

Jesus taught mutual edification in several ways. First, is
ministering to one another's material and spiritual needs. No
believer should ever think that they could live independent of
others or not need the help of others. The body of Christ—the
church—functions only as each member helps one another
through humility and gentleness (Gal. 6:1-2). The ministry of
the community is to "spur one another on toward love and good
deeds," and "let us not give up meeting together . . . but let us
encourage one another" (Heb. 10:24-25). This type of
atmosphere will encourage believers to confess their sins to one
another, faith and witness will flourish, and encourage one
another to become mature in the Lord (Eph. 4:13-16). We must
also "accept him whose faith is weak" and nurture them in the
Lord (Rom. 14:1, 19).

Second, it involves being accountable to one another. This
does not refer to blind obedience, but refers to living as one
body—being interrelated and interdependent upon each other.
Accountability is knowing that what each person does and how
each of us lives affects everyone within the community. On the
one hand, any willful, public sin as in the example of the
immoral brother (1 Cor. 5:1-13), hinders the proclamation of the

gospel. However, on the other hand, as we encourage and admonish one another we grow spiritually and the community as a whole benefits (Eph. 1:18) (Grenz 1996:221).

Third, Jesus taught mutual edification through prayer and intercession. According to Grenz, "prayer is a central means of mutual edification" (1996:221). We edify one another as we constantly pray and intercede for them. Each believer has the responsibility to function within the church as a priest. In the Old Testament, priests were responsible for praying, interceding, and offering sacrifices on behalf of the entire community. However, Jesus instituted the new priesthood of all believers, which entrusts every believer with the privilege of ministering to one another through prayer, edification, and love. Paul told the Romans "Let no debt remain outstanding, except the continuing debt to love one another, for he who loves his fellowman has fulfilled the law" (Rom. 13:8). One of the greatest examples of intercession is Jesus' intercession for His disciples (Jn. 17:15-17).

Implications for Today's Church

Dietrich Bonhoeffer in *Letters and Papers from Prison* said "The Church is the Church only when it exists for others" (1953:203). In the day in which we live, we need to reevaluate how the world sees the church and responds to it. The church today, unlike the Early Church, has lost its effectiveness in the world. Something is wrong when we no longer see "the gospel . . . as . . . the power of God for the salvation of everyone who believes: first for the Jew, then for the Gentile" (Rom. 1:16).

We no longer see the necessity of losing our lives for His sake and the sake of the gospel (Mt. 10:39). We have become too busy trying to find our life and at the same time we are losing our life and the lives of those we have been sent to reach with the gospel. In many ways the church has become an enemy to the sinner. Those who do not know Jesus Christ want to see His life lived out within the lives of His disciples, and since they only see dysfunction and disorder they do not want anything to do with the church. James states, "For where you have envy and selfish ambition, there you find disorder and every evil practice" (Jas. 3:16). This is a problem that is prevalent within the church today and unless we confront this envious and selfish ambition, we will not demonstrate to the world the life of Jesus Christ. This is a wake up call for the church, the body of Christ, to unite under the power and anointing of the Holy Spirit and turn our known world upside down like Paul and his companions (Acts 17:6).

The house church naturally developed out of the household structure.

> It was the hospitality of these homes which made possible the Christian worship, common meals, and courage-sustaining fellowship of the group. . . . These small fellowships were not dependent on conforming to temple or synagogue worship, nor on buildings they had erected. . . . The family-household basis must have had an overwhelming effect on the earliest believer's understanding of the church as family, the very "household of God" (Eph. 2:18-19; 3:14-15; 5:1; 6:23). Ultimately, as someone has said, every home should be a church, for a church is where Jesus dwells (Birkey 1988:54).

Fellowship within the Early Church was a natural expression of their love and appreciation for others. They understood and practiced what Jesus meant when He said "By this all men will know that you are my disciples, if you love one another" (Jn. 13:35). The key to this fellowship was the Holy Spirit who united each member for a common task, a common vision, the common good (1 Cor. 12:7). The unity of the Holy Spirit was naturally expressed as they viewed their possessions as belonging to all others (Acts 4:32).

Unlike society today, they were not preoccupied with material possessions, but viewed their possessions as the means for the edification of the community. This outward manifestation was founded upon an inner life transformed by the power of the Holy Spirit. This thought and purpose was their new nature in Jesus Christ, not something that required effort. The Early Church viewed fellowship as the highest priority and to them, "This is the church: persons who belong to each other and who support, serve, admonish, teach, and love each other without reservation or selfishness" (Gilliland 1998:186). If we today could only comprehend the ramifications of the fellowship of the Early Church it would transform our society like it transformed the community life of the Early Church.

The coming of the Holy Spirit at Pentecost was the means that made the evangelistic efforts the norm for the church and the reason for its existence. There is not a great emphasis on evangelism in the Early Church because it was the natural expression, gratitude, and pleasure to be witnesses of God's love that has been poured out into our heart by the Holy Spirit (Rom. 5:5).

> Such qualities of the church—fellowship and witness—are two sides of the same coin. They complement and enhance each other. The church that is in true fellowship in the Spirit is a witnessing church. The church that bears witness and thus sees the fruit of sharing of its own life is always richer in its fellowship (Gilliland 1998:189).

This fellowship only had meaning as it ministered in the world. Unless the church is in the world it ceases to be the church—the body of Christ. It is not enough just to fellowship with other believers. The essence of this fellowship is seen only as it is active in the world (society) (Van Engen 1991:126).

Throughout the Book of Acts, prayer, worship, fellowship was followed by a manifestation of God's power and being filled with the Holy Spirit, which resulted in the proclamation of the gospel (Acts 4:31; 6:1-7). Therefore, church growth was a natural expression of an inner conviction. It was not something, unlike today, that needed to be emphasized, studied, taught or theorized; it was simply done. I thank God for schools such as the School of World Mission at Fuller

Theological Seminary for helping students to understand church growth. However, we must go beyond this and be sensitive to the leading of the Holy Spirit if we are going to be effective in world evangelization.

Each member of the body of Christ has been chosen to a vital place of ministry within their local congregation. Each individual is so unique that no one else in the entire world has the same fingerprints, therefore, God has gifted each person to fulfill the task that He has gifted them to fulfill. Once each member of the body of Christ realizes this we will transform our society and community through the power of the Holy Spirit. The problem is that we leave the work up to someone else and in the meantime very little is being accomplished.

> Each local church is uniquely chosen by God to be His body in that place. His is an active body, with each member assigned a specific ministry to perform. In order to carry on those many ministries the church must organize itself for action in such a way that every member becomes active in ministry. It must pray for the Spirit of God to fill every member and anoint every ministry—then the church of the twentieth century will be revitalized, and not until then. . . . The Church cannot be fully the body of Christ, the people of God, unless it ministers in the world (Van Engen 1991:122, 126).

The Early Church began to develop leaders from the day they became members of the body of Christ, which taught them equality not a hierarchical pattern to ministry. In many of today's churches, there are so many classes, and programs that new believers must attend before they are qualified to become ministers of the gospel. Lawrence Richards and Gilbert Martin state,

> When we deny a clergy-laity distinction, we are affirming the *equality* of all believers! To some this seems a threatening doctrine. It appears to drag the clergy down to the level of the laity. In fact, equality in the church must be understood as lifting every believer up to realize his full potential as one of the *laos* of God! The basic reality on which this commitment is based is simply that each believer *is* equal: no distinction can be made between "first-class"

Christians (clergy) and "second-class" Christians (the laity) (1990:18).

We must return to the example of the Early Church if we are going to see our communities, societies, and world transformed. Church leadership must mobilize their members to be active participants within their communities and no longer pew warmers within the church.

Jesus commands His disciples (you and I) "So in everything, do to others what you would have them do to you, for this sums up the Law and the Prophets" (Mt. 7:12). We all desire what Jesus commanded us to do, and if we would only practice this, we would truly represent the community of love.

"A new command I give you: Love one another. As I have loved you, so you must love one another. By this all men will know that you are my disciples, if you love one another" (Jn. 13:34-35).

The church of Christ is by nature a family. It is in the reality of the family relationship that love is expressed and that the way of love is learned.

It's important to see the church as a fellowship within which people learn how to be loved and to love. Peter suggests that a genuine capacity to love comes from our relationship with God. "Now that you have purified yourselves by obeying the truth so that you have sincere love for your brothers," he says, "love one another deeply, from the heart" (1 Peter 1:22). *Our potential for loving is to be developed, by conscious effort, to a deep love and care for each other* (Richards and Martin 1990:196).

The dilemma is, why is something so simple, so difficult. Why is it so difficult to truly minister and edify others and in turn we ourselves are ministered to and edified. This was the key to the effectiveness of the Early Church, which was birthed in the coming, manifestation, and power of the Holy Spirit. Let us never forget that

Ministry is carrying out Christ's work in the world. . . . Ministry is the work of the church among its own members and in the world. It is carried out both corporately and individually and is not the exclusive responsibility of ordained ministers of the Word. In fact it is the work of all the people of God (Van Engen 1991:144).

Conclusion:

Abiding in Community

"Remain in me, and I will remain in you. No branch can bear fruit by itself; it must remain in the vine. Neither can you bear fruit unless you remain in me.

I am the vine; you are the branches. If a man remains in me and I in him, he will bear much fruit; apart from me you can do nothing. If anyone does not remain in me, he is like a branch that is thrown away and withers; such branches are picked up, thrown into the fire and burned. If you remain in me and my words remain in you, ask whatever you wish, and it will be given you. This is to my Father's glory, that you bear much fruit, showing yourselves to be my disciples.

As the Father has loved me, so have I loved you. Now remain in my love. If you obey my commands, you will remain in my love, just as I have obeyed my Father's commands and remain in his love. I have told you this so that my joy may be in you and that your joy may be complete. My command is this: Love each other as I have loved you. Greater love has no one than this, that he lay down his life for his friends. You are my friends if you do what I command. I no longer call you servants, because a servant does not know his master's business. Instead, I have called you friends, for everything that I learned from my Father I have made known to you. You did not choose me, but I chose you and appointed you to go and bear fruit—fruit that will last. Then the Father will give you whatever you ask in my name. This is my command: Love each other" (Jn. 15:4-17).

The same exhortation that is found here is similar to that found in the Book of Hebrews, where the Greek term μένω ("abide")[38] is found six times.[39] Just as the writer to the Hebrews seeks to keep them from stumbling when persecution

---

[38] The Greek term μένω (ménō) occurs 120 times in the New Testament, nearly half of which (55) appear in one of John's writings. The term occurs 34 times in the Gospel of John, 20 times in the Johannine epistles (18 times in 1 John, 2 times in 2 John), and once in Revelation.

[39] (7:3, 24; 10:34; 12:27; 13:1, 14).

intensifies against them, so our Lord speaks to His disciples in the Upper Room to keep them from stumbling (16:1) and to encourage them to abide in Him.

The apostle John uses the Greek verb μένω twelve times to demonstrate the abiding love of the heavenly community and how His body must abide in Him. Jesus gave His disciples five principles of how to abide in His love. First of all, when we abide in Him, we abide in the community of love (v. 4). Abiding in His love involves "cleansing" or pruning, which is painful for us at the time, but causes us to cling to the vine, and thus to bear more fruit, and this increased fruit is for His glory, as well as our good. It is not automatic; it is something which we are commanded to do, and which takes effort and action on our part. Abiding in Christ requires the self-discipline that Paul talks about (1 Cor. 9:24-27) and which the Holy Spirit produces (1 Tim. 1:7).

Second, when we abide in Him, we will keep His commandments (v. 10). Jesus gave us the greatest example of abiding in love by keeping His Father's commandments. Jesus never acted independently of the Father, even when Satan sought to tempt our Lord to do so in His testing in the wilderness (Mt. 4:1-11; Lk. 4:1-12). He spoke and did only what the Father told Him to speak and do (Jn. 8:29; 12:49-50). It is when we act independently of the community of love that we fail to maintain the vital connection necessary that sustains life. Not staying connected to the vine, the community of love results in bearing no fruit, because "without Me you can do nothing." Being a true disciple of Jesus Christ involves bearing fruit and if there is no lasting fruit, then there has not been a true connection to the vine.

Third, when we abide in Him, we will love our brothers and sisters who are also a part of the community of love. The greatest commandment that Jesus gave His disciples is to "love one another as I have loved you. Greater love has no one than this, than to lay down one's life for his friends" (Jn. 15:12-13).

Jesus also said that "Everyone will know by this that you are my disciples—if you have love for one another" (Jn. 13:34-35).

Fourth, when we abide in Him, we have great joy (v. 11). Jesus was emphasizing that joy should be the result of their new found life in Him, and that it logically follows that it is His life within them that is producing the fruit. Life within the community of love can only be filled with abundance, spontaneity, and joyfulness. Even though the disciples often experienced persecution, hardship, and distress, their joy was the result of His life living within them not on external circumstances. As we abide in Him our joy is really His joy; our life is really His life being transformed within us and through us.

Fifth, when we abide in Him, we are His friends (vv. 13-15). Jesus could not call His disciples friends until now because they were not prepared to think like Him, have the same goals, or motivations, even though He had communicated His mission to them. However, after the coming of the Holy Spirit, He could disclose His plans and purposes to them, because they were now prepared to fulfill His mission. Abiding in Christ intimately connects us with Him, so that we not only draw life and strength from Him, but we also come to know His heart and mind.

With the coming of the Holy Spirit on the Day of Pentecost, Jesus' disciples and every member of the body of Christ has Holy Spirit empowerment to bring transformation to the lives of others. Jesus said, "But you will receive power when the Holy Spirit comes on you; and you will be my witnesses in Jerusalem, and in all Judea and Samaria, and to the ends of the earth" (Acts 1:8). This is the power where ordinary people can bring about change in the lives of others. However, this power

Is found in connection, that profound meeting when the truest part of one soul meets the emptiest recesses in another and finds something there, when life passes from one to the other. When that happens, the giver is left more full than before and the receiver less terrified, eventually eager, to experience even deeper, more mutual connection. The power to meaningfully change lives depends not on advice, though counsel and rebuke play a part; not on insight, though self-awareness that disrupts complacency and points toward new understanding is important; but on connecting, on bringing two people into an experience of shared life (Crabb 1997:25).

This life is Jesus Christ being shared from one believer to another, from one denomination to another, from one church to another. This life crosses all national, cultural, linguistic, religious, racial boundaries, and transforms everything and everyone that opens the door and welcomes Him. The Early Church allowed the Holy Spirit to transform their lives, and equipped them to reach others with the gospel. We must believe that the gospel has given us life as we abide in Jesus Christ and then learn to release the power of that life within us so that we can nourish and nurture that life and goodness within others. As this happens, the healing process begins and damaged and broken lives are restored.

Within the body of Christ, we all have areas that need to be healed, whether it is broken homes and marriages, damaged relationships, or inner struggles, Jesus has already given us what we need to bring healing and restoration. All we need to do is cry out asking Him to fill us once again, and become connected to the source of all life. If we can only learn to listen, take time for others, show them how important they are to us, love them unconditionally, we will break the hold of Satan to destroy our lives and community. We need to tap into the powerful, dynamic, connecting force of the Holy Spirit who connects us to God, draws us to Jesus Christ and transforms our lives daily to be more like Him.

The deepest urge in every human heart is to be in relationship with someone who absolutely delights in us, someone with resources we lack who has no greater joy than giving to us, someone who respects us enough to require us to use everything we receive for the good of others, and because he has given it to us, knows we have something to give. The longing to connect defines our dignity as human beings and our destiny as image-bearers (Crabb 1997:38).

It is only as we give ourselves to others, open up to others, take risks and become vulnerable, that connection happens and healing takes place. We then realize that we are accepted and forgiven by others, courage develops and hope fills our hearts, life becomes enjoyable, and we are zealous for more intimate connection and giving ourselves to others. This is the only way to confront and bring restoration and reconciliation to the central problem within humanity, separation from God, from ourselves (dealing with our sin and hurt) and from others (demanding from others what we ourselves are unwilling to give).

Jesus has given us a choice, we can either live as unique members of a connected community where we experience daily the fruit of His life flowing through us to others or we can live as disconnected, desperate, empty, searching souls trying to fill the void that only He can fill. This search to be connected, was God's intention from the "foundations of the earth" (Ps. 102:25). True joy and happiness can only occur when we have surrendered our lives over to our Creator God and Savior, the Lord Jesus Christ.

> We were designed to connect with others: connecting is life. Loneliness is the ultimate horror. In connecting with God, we gain life. In connecting with others, we nourish and experience that life as we freely share it. Rugged individualism, proud independence, and chosen isolation violate the nature of our existence as much as trying to breathe under water. The capacities that distinguish us as human beings from all other creations (including angels and animals) were given to us so we could connect with each other the way the three divine persons connect. We have the capacity to enjoy the wonder of a relationship built on grace that no angel has ever personally experienced (fallen angels are not forgiven and unfallen one's don't need to be). Combine that capacity with the capacities to think, imagine, aspire, choose, and feel, and you have people built for trinitarian-like community. . . . The life of Christ is coming out of me only when I am gladly ruled by a passion to know you, to bless you, and to be known by you so that together we can enjoy fellowship with Christ and with each other (Crabb 1997:45).

As Jesus was sent by the community of love as God incarnate into this world, so likewise we have been sent as His body incarnate into this world to exalt Him. "But I, when I am lifted up from the earth, will draw all men to myself" (Jn. 12:32). More than ever the body of Christ needs Jesus, to be His body incarnate in this world. The only Jesus that the world will see is the Jesus that is manifested in and through us. If Jesus does not have His rightful place in our lives how will He take His rightful place as the King of Kings and Lord of Lords in this world and unbelievers will be drawn to Him.

The Purpose of the Church's Existence

God has an eternal purpose for the church that began with creation and ended with the redemption of humankind. This purpose was manifested in and through Jesus Christ, which is the church. There is nothing that can frustrate the purposes of God through Jesus Christ and His church (Eph. 3). The church that Jesus instituted in the early 1st century was built upon the pattern established in the Old Testament in the tabernacle in the wilderness. The purpose of the church's existence is fourfold. The first three are patterned after the Old Testament model and fourth is added from the New Testament.

The primary purpose of the church is to glorify and worship God. All ministry is first of all directed to the Lord. All of creation was designed by God for His pleasure (Rev. 4:11). God created the church through Jesus Christ to be a worshipping community (Ps. 29:1-2). The body of Christ has been redeemed to offer up praise and worship to God and then to serve Him from hearts filled with joy and thanksgiving. This worship can only come from hearts full of the Spirit and truth from the Word of God (Jn. 4:23). In the Old Testament this is seen as the high priest would enter the Holy of Holies once a year to atone for the sins of the people (Lev. 16).

The second purpose of the church is to minister to one another. We have been called to edify, minister to one another,

to build one another up in love (Eph. 4:9-16, 1 Cor. 12). As we
minister unto one another we provide a covering and protection
for them against every attack from the enemy. The third
purpose of the church is to minister to the sinner. We have been
called with a purpose, which is to minister the gospel of Jesus
Christ to the sinner. The more effective our ministry is to the
Lord, the more effective our ministry will be to one another, and
therefore the more effective our ministry will be to those who
do not know Jesus Christ as their personal Savior. If only the
world could see the true Christian life, it would revolutionize
the church's ministry in our communities. We have been called
to minister like Jesus who came "to seek and to save what was
lost" (Lk. 19:10).

The fourth and final purpose of the church is a ministry of
conquering Satan and his demonic forces. Jesus called His
church to be militant and triumphant where even "the gates of
Hades will not overcome it" (Mt. 16:18). The church that Jesus
instituted will be a victorious church, clothed with the power,
the armor of God and the spiritual weapons of warfare (Eph.
6:10-20, 2 Cor. 10:1-5). The Early Church demonstrated these
fourfold purposes of the church's existence and through this
they were an effective witness of Jesus Christ. On the Day of
Pentecost Peter opened the door of the gospel to the Jews (Acts
2) and then opened this same door to the Gentiles in Acts 10-11.
The ministry of the Early Church was a continuation of the
ministry Jesus inaugurated and with His blood He "purchased
men for God from every tribe and language and people and
nation" (Rev. 5:9).

Missiological Implications

The missiological implications for the church today can be
seen in the overall attitude that was felt within and through the
Early Church. This prevalent attitude was demonstrated in that
everything they did was done in "one accord" (Acts 1:14; 2:1,
46; 4:24; 5:12). They were a unified body of believers who

ministered under the power and anointing of the Holy Spirit, which sums up the community life of the Early Church. The concept of unity in the Early Church was their greatest expression of the gospel of Jesus Christ. They saw that since God is one (Dt. 6:4-5), there is one gospel, and therefore one church which Jesus Christ is the Head (Eph. 5:23, Col. 1:18).

The concept of one inclusive unified community is found in two key passages in the teaching of Jesus. The first one is His teaching on the Good Shepherd (Jn. 10:1-18), and the second is His high priestly prayer (Jn. 17). Both references indicate that there is one church as He uses the metaphor of a shepherd to describe His relationship with His followers and in the latter, indicates one unified collected body of believers. The key thought in both references, is the expression of "love" in this one community. Jesus conceived of all His disciples as being "one people." Jesus emphasized relational unity and mutual support with this unified community. The singular concept of "church" included all those who had an underlying unity of faith that connected all believers to Jesus Christ.

The New Testament teaching on unity within the church, first of all, is seen as a relational unity, which involved love and harmony, and not organizational unity or external connectedness. In reference to unity within the church, Jesus desires that the key characteristic of His people would be a unity of love. Jesus prays that His disciples would be unified after the pattern exemplified between the Father and the Son.

> "My prayer is not for them alone. I pray also for those who will believe in me through their message, that all of them may be one, Father, just as you are in me and I am in you. May they also be in us so that the world may believe that you have sent me. I have given them the glory that you gave me, that they may be one as we are one: I in them and you in me. May they be brought to complete unity to let the world know that you sent me and have loved them even as you have loved me" (Jn. 17:20-23).

The second New Testament teaching on unity focuses on unity being grounded on foundational Christian doctrine or truth. This is a shared faith where all who believe in Jesus Christ have also become one in faith. The apostle Paul emphasizes in Ephesians 4:4-6 that Christian unity within the church is founded upon "one faith" because without this faith there would be no need for a relational unity to exist among them.

> "There is one body and one Spirit—just as you were called to one hope when you were called—one Lord, one faith, one baptism; one God and Father of all, who is over all and through all and in all" (Eph. 4:4-6).

Jesus knew that as the church grew that temperaments, backgrounds, and interests would also become more diverse. He emphasized the need for His body to remain unified not based upon any external opinion or uniformity, but on their new nature of being a member of the family of God. Authentic love and unity within His body, the church was His greatest passion.

Likewise today, Jesus' passion for love and unity within His church is still a high priority. We need to comprehend the community life of the Early Church and implement its characteristics into our society today. It is time that we become and function as one like the community of love is and functions as one. When this is happening every man-made boundary that has ever existed will be broken down. We will no longer see division between denominations, even though what we believe is important to us, it will not hinder our calling and purpose as a united body of Christ. The use of denominational titles will no longer be a place of security since we will know who we are in Jesus Christ and our place within His body. When we truly are functioning as His body incarnate, division between churches and its members will be no more, because we will recognize a higher calling as His ambassadors.

I pray that you have heard my heart and also the voice of the Lord encouraging you to put aside and forgive whatever

differences you may have between yourself and another fellow
member of the body of Christ. I also pray that any issue you
may have with another denomination or church that you will
seek to reconcile these issues in order that the gospel may once
again be "the power of God for the salvation of everyone who
believes: first for the Jew, then for the Gentile" (Rom. 1:16).
As the old cliché says, since we are going to live together as a
community in heaven, we better start to live like one here on
earth. It is time that we truly become the community of love
that we were created to reflect and function as true brothers and
sisters in the Lord.

The song below is the cry of my heart for the body of
Christ.

"We Need Jesus"

When will the world see that we need Jesus?
If we open our eyes we will all realize that He loves us.
When will the world see that we need Jesus?
When our hearts are as one
and believe that He's the Son of our God.

The Lord is our God
and we shall never want
The Lord is our God
and we shall live forever.
When we share the love of Jesus
See each other as He sees us.
Then His love will see us through
His love will see us through.

When will the world see that we need Jesus?
When sister and brother love one another as one.
When will the world see that we need Jesus?
Will we ever understand Jesus is the Son of man?
We must live in the shadow of His love.

When will the world see that we need Jesus?
If we open our eyes we will all realize that He loves us.
When will the world see that we need Jesus?
When our hearts are as one
and believe that He's the Son of our God.

When will the world see that we need Jesus?
When sister and brother love one another as one.
When will the world see that we need Jesus?
Will we ever understand Jesus is the Son of man?
We must live in the shadow of His love.

"We Need Jesus" Petra
(Elefante, Elefante, and Springer 1990)

Appendix A:

The Community of Love
in the Old Testament

"May God Almighty bless you and make you fruitful and increase your numbers until you become a community of peoples. May he give you and your descendants the blessing given to Abraham, so that you may take possession of the land where you now live as an alien, the land God gave to Abraham" (Gen. 28:3-4).

"And God said to him, 'I am God Almighty; be fruitful and increase in number. A nation and a community of nations will come from you, and kings will come from your body. The land I gave to Abraham and Isaac I also give to you, and I will give this land to your descendants after you'" (Gen. 35:11-12).

God desired from the beginning a community of people who would be fruitful and increase in numbers. This community would continue and include descendents from all generations. This is seen throughout the Old Testament with its establishment under the headship of Jesus Christ in the New Testament.

Old Testament Definition

The noun used for community in the Old Testament is *qahal* (קָהָל) and refers to the assembling of a group of people without regard to its purpose; an assembly for religious purposes. It is usually translated in the LXX as ἐκκλησία, also as συναγωγὴ thirty-six times. It also refers to the community of angels (Ps. 89:5). It may designate

Evil council or deeds (Gen. 49:6; Ps. 26:5), civil affairs (1 Kings 2:3; Pr. 5:14; 26:26; Job 30:28), or war (Num. 22:4; Jud. 20:2 . . . . an assembled multitude of nations (Gen. 35:11), peoples (Gen. 28:3; 48:4) and even the dead (Pr. 21:16). It may also be of the returning exiles (Jer. 31:8; Ezra 2:64), and then the restored community in

175

Israel (Ezra 10:12, 14; Neh. 8:2) (Harris, Archer, and Waltke 1980:790).

The Israelite experience at Mount Horeb and the receiving of the Law was "the day of assembly" (Dt. 9:10; 10:4; 18:16). There were also many other occasions when the community was called together: feasts, fasts, and worship (2 Ch. 20:5; 30:25; Neh. 5:13; Joel 2:16). These references refer to only a portion of the community of Israel gathering together and at other times particular Israelite's were prohibited to enter the community. Lastly, *qahal* refers to the community as an organized body (Ex. 12:6; Jud. 20:2; Dt. 31:30; Num. 16:3; Neh. 13:1) (Harris, Archer, and Waltke 1980:790).

The Community of Love and Joseph

One of the greatest narratives concerning community in the Old Testament is found in the story of Joseph in Genesis 37-50. This story provides the first stage in the transition from a patriarchal family to an independent nation. Joseph, who was the youngest son of Jacob, was spoiled and hated by his older brothers. "The Midianites sold Joseph in Egypt to Potiphar, one of Pharaoh's officials, the captain of the guard" (Gen. 37:36). Joseph's God-given leadership abilities of virtue, wisdom, and grace are used to interpret Pharaoh's troubling dreams and through this he is appointed a high administrative office under Pharaoh's leadership (Gen. 40-41). Joseph's position opens the door for him to provide for his family during a severe famine by bringing them to Egypt (Gen. 42-47) (LaSor, Hubbard, and Bush 1996:48).

Joseph's betrayal by his brothers plays a key role in the establishment of a chosen people. The children of Israel were for a period of time an isolated and protected community who dwelt in the land of Goshen, also known as the northeastern Nile delta. The "survival of a numerous people" (Gen. 50:20,

RSV) makes reference to the narrative of the exodus and ultimately to the future deliverance through Jesus Christ.

Personally, the story of Joseph, is very significant since it brings to remembrance the rejection that I faced as a young boy. At the age of three years old, I was scolded with boiling water and still have on my back and legs the third degree scars from this accident. My classmates and others would see these scars, make fun of me, and call me names. Like Joseph, who showed love and acceptance to his brothers even though they hated and rejected him, I learned to love and accept other people as they are and not allow our differences to become a barrier that separates us. Love and acceptance play a major role in the formation of community, which has been a vital aspect of the ministry that God has called me to fulfill.

Joseph, as a foreigner was maligned and imprisoned (Gen. 37-39), and treated as an outcast. He lived the life of the poor and understood how they felt. Through this experience he developed a heart of love, acceptance and compassion for the less fortunate. Through all of this, the Lord has given me a heart for those who are treated as outcasts and to show them that God has an everlasting love and accepts them in their present condition. People do not care how much you know, but they do want to know how much you care.

The Community of Love in Judges 20

The primary focus of the Book of Judges is the breakdown or complete collapse of the religious life of Israel. Judges can be divided into three sections. First of all, the first sixteen chapters explain their failure in not keeping the covenant and their failure in the conquest (1:1-2:5). Second, by the repeated cycle of sin, judgment, repentance, and deliverance (2:6-16:31). Third, the final result of their failure in the total collapse of a society into a chaotic lifestyle (17-21). In this final section, unlike the first sixteen chapters, no judges are named, no enemies to confront, and no outside danger threatens them. It also describes the perversion and corruption of this time, which is contrasted with the peaceful period of the later monarchies.

Chapter 19 describes how a series of human weaknesses can result in a national disaster, which begins with the unfaithfulness of a Levite's concubine who is later reconciled with her husband. The Levite goes to bring home his concubine and her father persuades him into staying for five days. The Levite's lack of determination to return home to his business affairs results in leaving late in the afternoon, and refusing to stay with a Gentile Jebustite is ironic. They were not Israelites and he wanted to find lodging in Gibeah where he would expect to be shown good hospitality. Even though both Jebus and Gibeah belonged to the tribe of Benjamin, their immorality was well known. The entire community of Gibeah had chosen to tolerate immoral practices rather than confronting and judging its sin.

The climax of their journey begins when they have to wait for lodging and finally an Ephraimite invites them to stay for the night. Then, suddenly "the wicked men of the city" (19:22) demand that this Ephraimite bring out the Levite to commit a homosexual act. Instead, the Levite sent out his concubine where she is raped and murdered because they wanted to kill him. "This night of horror made a powerful impact on the nation, and centuries later the prophet Hosea recalled the depth of Gibeah's corruption (Hos. 9:9; 10:9)" (Gaebelein 1992, 3:493).

The devastating rape and murder influenced the Levite to take drastic action. "He cut up her body as one divides the carcass of a sacrificial animal (Ex. 29:17; Lev. 1:6)" and distributes equal parts to the twelve tribes of Israel, especially to the leaders of the tribe of Benjamin. This same technique was used at Gibeah by King Saul, who cut up oxen and circulated them throughout Israel to raise an army (1 Sam. 11:7). The Israelites reacted with burning indignation and were repulsed by this act. This hideous crime united Israel against the tribe of Benjamin to the place where they rise up as "one man" (אִישׁ אֶחָד)

with one sword. This phrase is used three times in chapter 20 (vv. 1, 8, 11) and "stresses unity while recognizing diversity within that oneness . . . also refers to a nation aroused to take united action against gross injustice (Jud. 20:8; 1 Sam. 11:7)" (Harris, Archer, and Waltke 1980:30). It does not appear that the Israelites on this occasion, were summoned by the authority of any one common head, but they came together by the consent and agreement of one common heart, fired with a holy zeal for the honour of God and Israel.

The Israelites brought men from every corner of Israel to assemble at Mizpah, which was "an old shrine (1 Sam. 7:5; 10:17) . . . in the territory of Benjamin (Jos. 18:26)" (Buttrick 1953, 2:815). The Levite pleads for justice with "the people of God" (20:2) who respond by asking the leaders of Gibeah to surrender "the wicked men of the city" to be punished for their crime which was death. Capital punishment was prescribed so that these idolaters and rebellious men could be purged from Israel (Dt. 13:5; 21:21). However, the leaders of Gibeah chose to be loyal to their men and a punitive operation against Gibeah ended in a civil war.

Three battles now occur and Israel loses the first since they were at a disadvantage to the skilled Benjaminite's in the hilly terrain. This first defeat brought Israel to their knees maybe because the result of national sin or attacking a "brother" tribe. The second battle again brought defeat and now 22,000 men from the first battle were "cut down" (20:21) and another 18,000 men from the second battle were "cut down" (20:25) for a total of 40,000 men or ten percent of their army. They retreated to Bethel, which was eight miles north of Gibeah where they wept, fasted, and offered burnt and fellowship offerings, which expressed devotion and commitment. "In the ancient Near East, the third time for any event was often a decisive time" (Gaebelein 1992, 3:499).

This time, however, God had given them a strategy, which was an ambush and had also been successful at Ai (Jos. 8:2) and also at Shechem by Abimelech (Jud. 9:33-44). While the

Israelites were retreating to the north and the army from Gibeah was pursuing them, the rest of the Israelite army ambushed the city of Gibeah and set it on fire signaling victory and the capture of the city. The only thing that remained was the surviving Benjaminite's amazement at the outcome and they flee for their lives. They "were terrified" (20:41) compares with the shock that Joseph's brothers felt when they realized that he was still alive (Gen. 45:3).

No matter where the Benjaminites fled, the Israelites pursued them until "the rock of Rimmon," but 600 men escaped and stayed at Rimmon for four months. Meanwhile, the Israelites returned to the land of Benjamin and killed the inhabitants of every town, even the animals, and set them on fire. This was done in accordance to Deuteronomy 13:12-18, which states that any Israelite city that harbored idolaters was to be burned, both people and animals. The sin of Gibeah was considered as serious as idolatry.

Israel won this battle against the Benjaminites because they stood together and fought as "one man" with one sword. Even though these tribes were comprised of various villages and clans within each tribe, and composed of extended and nuclear families their social structure was more egalitarian than hierarchical. This was a prime example of what is called "strength in numbers." "Archaeological evidence from the early Iron Age suggests that 'highland villages reflect the essential social structure of early Israel—almost precisely as the Book of Judges . . . has faithfully preserved it in the written record'" (LaSor, Hubbard, and Bush 1996:160).

In the life of Joseph, we saw the positive aspects of community life and now in Judges chapter 20, we have negative aspects as seen in the community of Benjamin. The Israelites joined together as "one man" to adhere to the law of God and purge the immorality of the Benjaminites from the land. However, on the other hand, the Benjaminites united together to preserve their *immoral* community life. The point that it being made here is that we need to make sure that we are following the Lord's leading in everything we do, because if we wander from it there are consequences that we will need to face. Like the Levite, I have at times lacked determination, which has resulted in difficult circumstances. Even though I learned valuable lessons, there were still consequences that remained for some time.

The Community of Love in Nehemiah 5-8

Nehemiah was a leader of the Jewish community who returned to Palestine with Zerubbabel approximately 538 B.C., which was the end of the Babylonian exile. Some scholars believe that Ezra reestablished Israel's spirituality through rebuilding the temple, and Nehemiah gave this fragile community physical stability in the midst of opposition. Nehemiah through God-given wisdom and unselfish disposition brought new life into this dying Jewish community in Jerusalem. He brought physical stability through the rebuilding of the city walls, socially through helping the poor and oppressed, and nationally by placing the law of Moses in its proper place (Buttrick 1962, 3:534). According to Ezra and Nehemiah, the temple was the highest importance, and then the purification of the Jewish community, which is described in the Book of Ezra. Next, the rebuilding of the city wall and finally the climax of the reading of the law. Nehemiah chapters 8-9 refer to the conclusion of the restoration.

As Nehemiah comes on the scene he sees a disadvantaged class which no one seems to care about. If the situation should continue, the community would be in danger of splitting apart and the work of the wall would stop. Here we have unjust economic inequities among the Jewish people. The rich (nobles and officials) were oppressing the poor by making them mortgage their property and borrow money in order to buy food. Some were forced to give their children as slaves to keep from starving. Nehemiah rose up in anger and brought the offenders to repentance and correction.

When Nehemiah hears about the protest of the poor he becomes extremely angry and charges the Nobles and Officials with "exacting usury from your own countrymen" (5:7) which was a violation of the legislation in Exodus 22:25. He also states that whenever a Jewish slave was offered for sale in a Gentile marketplace, he would pay the ransom and set them free. These Nobles and Officials knowing this continued to sell these slaves which was morally wrong, and also that they should "walk in the fear of our God to avoid reproach of our Gentile enemies" (5:9). The Nobles and Officials agree to Nehemiah's plea and he "shook out the folds of my robe" (5:13) which emphasized "may God shake out of his house and possessions every man who does not keep this promise" (5:13). It was known that a governor or ruler was expected to entertain lavishly which was social responsibility. However, Nehemiah was known for his generosity. "The generosity of Nehemiah as of wealthy Bedouin sheiks is felt to consist in the fact that they let any number of poor relations come to dinner" (Gaebelein 1988, 4:710).

Sanballat and Geshem send Nehemiah a message in an attempt to entice him out of the city to "one of the villages on the plain of Ono" (6:2) which was about twenty miles Northwest of Jerusalem. He realized that this invitation was a dangerous tactic to hinder the completion of the wall and refuses to leave. These three opposers had earlier tried to stop the building of the wall through ridicule (4:1-6) and terrorist attacks (4:7-23) had proved ineffective. Sanballat does not give up in his plot against Nehemiah's life through four attempts, who refuses on all accounts.

Sanballat on his fifth attempt, accuses Nehemiah and the Jews of planning a rebellion against Artaxerxes of Persia proclaiming himself as king and everyone who handled the letter would read it and spread its message. The final strategy of Nehemiah's enemies was when Tobiah and Sanballat bribes a prophet named Shemaiah to prophesy to Nehemiah to seek shelter within the temple because of the threat against his life.

Nehemiah refuses because (1) he is not a priest and would violate the sanctity of the temple; (2) he would not place his own personal safety above that of his fellow Jews. There were many other false prophets who tried to intimidate Nehemiah (6:14, 18), but he stood firm because he knew the task that God had called him to accomplish (Laymon 1971:229). Nehemiah prays that God would remember his faithfulness and his enemies be punished for their attempts to hinder the rebuilding of the wall.

The rebuilding of the temple under Ezra's leadership took twenty-two years primarily because after they began the construction, the Jews became discouraged and stopped working until Haggai and Zechariah prophesied to them. The rebuilding of the wall under Nehemiah's leadership only took fifty-two days. The success of the project was a witness to "all the surrounding nations" (6:16) and enemies who finally realized that since God was behind this work, nothing or no one could hinder its completion. Even though the wall has been completed, Tobiah remains apart of this Jewish community because of his marriage into an eminent Jewish family who gives him contact with many leaders in Judah (Freedman 1992, 6:584).

Nehemiah now takes security precautions by appointing two men, his brother Hanani and Hananiah "the commander of the citadel" (7:2) to be in charge over Jerusalem. He states the time each day that the gates will be open and closed and also that guards be appointed to protect private homes. He also attempts to encourage some of the Jews who had established themselves in the surrounding area to relocate inside the city walls. He finds a genealogy of the first families to return from the Babylonian exile and begins the process of repopulating the city.

It is interesting that "all the people assembled as one man" (8:1) is almost verbatim to Judges 20:1, 8, 11, and speaks of a united community posed for action. As the people listen to the law of Moses, read daily from the first day of the Feast of

Booths to the last day, a revival breaks out where there is weeping because of their sins and later punishment because of mixed marriages.

I appreciate how the Jews united with one common purpose in mind when they needed to confront a specific task. As the body of Christ unites the power of the gospel will have a greater effect in a shorter period of time. When the church becomes as "one man" then the power of the gospel be ultimately displayed. As Jesus said "A new command I give you: Love one another. As I have loved you, so you must love one another. By this all men will know that you are my disciples, if you love one another" (Jn. 13:34-35).

Appendix B:

Servanthood in the
Old Testament

Jesus is the prominent Old Testament servant, who promised to perform the will of God perfectly and free the captives. Jesus is beautifully portrayed as the servant of the Lord, His relationship with God, and His attitude in ministry in Isaiah 42:1-4.

> "Here is my servant, whom I uphold, my chosen one in whom I delight; I will put my Spirit on him and he will bring justice to the nations. He will not shout or cry out, or raise his voice in the streets. A bruised reed he will not break, and a smoldering wick he will not snuff out. In faithfulness he will bring forth justice; he will not falter or be discouraged till he establishes justice on earth. In his law the islands will put their hope."

Jesus exemplified the life of a servant, which was not an attractive lifestyle. It required a high cost. Jesus is portrayed as the servant of all, in the Book of Isaiah.

> The Servant was chosen by the Lord (42:1; 49:1) and endued with the Spirit (42:1); He was taught by the Lord (50:4), and found His strength in Him (49:2, 5). It was the Lord's will that he should suffer (53:10); He was weak, unimpressive, and scorned by men (52:14; 53:1-3, 7-9), meek (42:2), gentle (42:3), and uncomplaining (50:6; 53:7). Despite His innocence (53:9), He was subjected to constant suffering (50:6; 53:3, 8-10), so as to be reduced to near-despair (49:4). But His trust was in the Lord (49:4; 50:7-9); He obeyed Him (50:4-5), and persevered (50:7) until He was victorious (42:4; 50:8, 9) (Tenney 1975, 5:361).

Jesus' mission was to Israel, which involved bringing this rebellious nation to repentance and back to God (Isa. 49:5). His mission extended to bringing judgment and salvation and being the light to the nations, which was accomplished through His life, death, burial, and resurrection (Isa. 42:1, 3-4; 49:6; 53:4-8). Servanthood in the Old Testament was considered a high and special calling, which involved a covenantal relationship with God. This relationship consisted of a willing commitment to the Master who likewise commits Himself to the servant (Tenney 1975, 5:361).

We can see the servant/master relationship in Leviticus 25 and Exodus 21. In Leviticus 25, we can see how an Israelite who became poor and sells himself to a fellow Israelite who is wealthy, can never serve as a slave

> "If one of your countrymen becomes poor among you and sells himself to you, do not make him work as a slave. He is to be treated as a hired worker or a temporary resident among you; he is to work for you until the Year of Jubilee" (Lev. 25:39-40).

However, in Exodus, the slave on his own free will could choose to remain a slave for life

> "But if the servant declares, 'I love my master and my wife and children and do not want to go free,' then his master must take him before the judges. He shall take him to the door or the doorpost and pierce his ear with an awl. Then he will be his servant for life" (Ex. 21:5-6).

The parallel described here shows our emptiness and poverty of life that we choose to live, but now we can serve a God of unlimited resources for the rest of our life. We have been called by God who shapes us to be the leaders of His body, and serve Him wherever He chooses to place us. Our service to God and to others is dependent upon our love for God and others.

Appendix C:

Old Testament Priesthood

The first recorded reference to the priesthood is in Genesis 14:18, speaks of Abram and his return from battle meets two kings; Bera, the King of Sodom who was a wicked king, and Melchizedek, who was King of Salem and a righteous king and "a priest of God Most High." Priest-King Melchizedek blesses Abram for his victory, and gives Melchizedek "a tenth of everything" (Gen. 14:20).

The covenant that God made between Himself and Israel they were seen as a "kingdom of priests" and therefore a Holy people (Ex. 19:6). Within this "kingdom of priests," three orders existed—the offices of the high priest, the priest, and the Levite. The priests were male descendents of Aaron (Num. 3:10), and the Levites were male members of the tribe of Levi.

Their primary duties were in the temple where they were responsible for the ceremonial vessels, performed the sacrifices, and various other duties. The high priest was head of all spiritual functions of Israel and was the only one allowed to enter the Holy of Holies on the Day of Atonement (Lev. 16). The Levites assisted the priests and served the community by performing various duties within the temple. They were in charge of the worship, cleaned the temple, assisted the priests in the preparation of certain sacrifices and offerings, and also taught.

The church becoming a priesthood of all believers was an Old Testament prophecy that was fulfilled at the coming of Jesus, " And you will be called priests of the Lord, you will be named ministers of our God" (Isa. 61:6). The new community of believers saw these prophecies fulfilled and people from all nations are called to belong to the chosen, Holy, priesthood of God.

Appendix D:

The Nicene Creed

I believe in one God the Father Almighty; Maker of heaven and earth, and of all things visible and invisible.

And in one Lord Jesus Christ, the only begotten of the Father before all worlds, Light of Light, very God of very God, begotten, not made, being of one substance with the Father; by whom all things were made; who, for us men and for our salvation, came down from heaven, and was incarnate by the Holy Spirit of the Virgin Mary, and was made man; and was crucified also for us under Pontius Pilate; he suffered and was buried; and the third day he rose again, according to the Scriptures; and ascended into heaven, and sitteth on the right hand of the Father; and he shall come again, with glory, to judge both the quick and the dead; whose kingdom shall have no end.

And in the Holy Spirit, the Lord and Giver of Life; who proceedeth from the Father; who with the Father and the Son together is worshipped and glorified; who spake by the Prophets. And in one Holy Catholic and Apostolic Church. I acknowledge one Baptism for the remission of sins; and I look for the resurrection of the dead, and the life of the world to come. Amen (Schaff 1985, 2:58).

Glossary

Kaddish A word meaning "Sanctification," and the name of prayer written in Aramaic (Bridger 1976:259). In this later function it is commonly recited by the mourner at the grave-side of parents or close relatives, and during the three daily prayers in the synagogue for the first eleven months following the death of a parent or relative. The Kaddish has no direct reference to the dead or to the mourning. It is essentially a doxology, praising God, and praying for the speedy establishment of God's Kingdom on earth, and is to this day recited by the Reader several times during each public service (Bridger 1976:259).

Shema One of the oldest and most important Hebrew prayers. Deriving its name from its first word, the *Shema* is held to be in a sense Israel's affirmation of faith: "Hear, O Israel, the Lord our God, the Lord is One." When the *Shema* is recited in the morning and evening services, it is accompanied by the reading of three other selections from the Pentateuch. Before retiring, only the first paragraph *(Veahavta)* is read. The reform practice is to be read only the one paragraph even at services (Bridger 1976:445). The Jewish confession of faith made up of Deut. 6:4-9 and 11:13-21 and Num. 15:37-41 (Mish 1993:1080).

Shemone Esre (shemoneh 'esreh, which means eighteen, with the word *berachoth*, "benedictions," understood), designation for the principal supplicatory prayer of the Jewish liturgy, for which reason it is called Tefillah ("prayer") in old Jewish sources. (shemoneh 'esreh, which means eighteen, with the word *berachoth*, 'benedictions,' understood), designation for the principal supplicatory prayer of the Jewish liturgy, for which reason it is called Tefillah ("prayer") in old Jewish sources. Since it is recited while the worshippers are standing, it is frequently called *'Amidah* ("standing"), especially among Sephardic Jews. The name Eighteen Benedictions is derived from the fact that at the time of its redaction the prayer consisted of eighteen paragraphs, each one of which concluded with a benediction and with one of the characteristic attributes of God (*hathimah*, "conclusion"; such as *hathimah* is usually called "eulogy" or "praise of God" in the liturgy) (Landman 1941, 4:22).

189

References Cited

Achtemeier, Paul J., ed.
1985   *Harper's Bible Dictionary.* First edition. San
Francisco, CA: Harper and Row, Publishers.

Adams, Jay E.
1986   *Handbook of Church Discipline.* Grand Rapids, MI:
Zondervan Publishing House.

Adamson, James B.
1976   *The Epistle of James.* Grand Rapids, MI: William B.
Eerdmans Publishing Company.

Aland, Kurt
1985   *A History of Christianity.* James L. Schaaf, trans.
Philadelphia, PA: Fortress Press.

Allen, Roland
1960   *The Spontaneous Expansion of the Church: And the
Causes That Hinder It.* Fourth edition. London:
World Dominion Press.

Baker, Robert A.
1959   *A Summary of Christian History.* Nashville, TN:
Broadman and Holman Publishers.

Balz, Horst, and Gerhard Schneider, eds.
1990   *Exegetical Dictionary of the New Testament.* Vols. 2-
3. Grand Rapids, MI: William B. Eerdmans Publishing
Company.

Banks, Robert
1994   *Paul's Idea of Community: The Early House Churches
in their Cultural Setting.* Revised edition. Peabody,
MA: Hendrickson Publishers.

Barrett, C. K.
1994   *A Critical and Exegetical Commentary on The Acts of
the Apostles.* Vol. 1. Edinburgh, Scotland: T. and T.
Clark Ltd.

Barrett, Lois
1986   *Building the House Church.* Scottsdale, PA: Herald
Press.

Barth, Karl
   1958   *Church Dogmatics.* Vol. 4. G. T. Thomson, trans.
          Edinburgh, UK: T. and T. Clark.
Bauckham, Richard, ed.
   1995   *The Book of Acts in its Palestinian Setting.* Grand
          Rapids, MI: William B. Eerdmans Publishing
          Company.
Birkey, Del
   1988   *The House Church: A Model for Renewing the Church.*
          Scottsdale, PA: Herald Press.
Bonhoeffer, Dietrich
   1953   *Letters and Papers from Prison.* New York:
          Macmillian.
Bounds, E. M.
   1984   *The Necessity of Prayer.* Springdale, PA: Whitaker
          House.
Bridger, David. ed.
   1976   *The New Jewish Encyclopedia.* New York: Behrman
          House.
Bromiley, Geoffrey W., ed.
   1974   *Theological Dictionary of the New Testament.* Vol. 9.
          Grand Rapids, MI: William B. Eerdmans Publishing
          Company.
   1982   *The International Standard Bible Encyclopedia.* Vol.
          2. Grand Rapids, MI: William B. Eerdmans Publishing
          Company.
   1985   *Theological Dictionary of the New Testament:
          Abridged in One Volume.* Grand Rapids, MI: William
          B. Eerdmans Publishing Company.
Brown, Colin, ed.
   1978   *The New International Dictionary of New Testament
          Theology.* Vol. 3. Grand Rapids, MI: Zondervan
          Publishing House.
   1986   *The New International Dictionary of New Testament
          Theology.* Vols. 1-2. Grand Rapids, MI: Zondervan
          Publishing House.

Bruce, F. F.
  1988   *The Book of Acts.* Revised edition. Grand Rapids, MI:
        William B. Eerdmans Publishing Company.
Bruce, F. F., ed.
  1986   *The International Bible Commentary.* Grand Rapids,
        MI: Zondervan Publishing House.
Buttrick, George A., ed.
  1951   *The Interpreter's Bible.* Vol. 7. New York: Abingdon-
        Cokesbury Press.
  1952   *The Interpreter's Bible.* Vol. 8. New York: Abingdon-
        Cokesbury Press.
  1953   *The Interpreter's Bible.* Vol. 2. New York: Abingdon-
        Cokesbury Press.
  1962   *The Interpreter's Dictionary of the Bible.* Vols. 1 and
        3. New York: Abingdon Press.
Cairns, Earle E.
  1996   *Christianity Through the Centuries: A History of the
        Christian Church.* 3rd edition. Revised and expanded.
        Grand Rapids, MI: Zondervan Publishing House.
Cassidy, Richard J.
  1978   *Jesus, Politics, and Society: A Study of Luke's Gospel.*
        Maryknoll, NY: Orbis Books.
Clinton, J. Robert
  1988   *The Making of a Leader.* Colorado Springs, CO:
        NavPress Publications.
Crabb, Larry
  1997   *Connecting: Healing For Ourselves and Our
        Relationships.* Nashville, TN: Word Publishing.
Davids, Peter H.
  1990   *The First Epistle of Peter.* Grand Rapids, MI: William
        B. Eerdmans Publishing Company.
Douglas, J. D., ed.
  1962   *New Bible Dictionary.* Second edition. Wheaton, IL:
        Tyndale House Publishers.

Drane, John W.
  1992 *Introducing the New Testament.* San Francisco, CA:
        Harper and Row Publishers.
Dunn, James D. G.
  1988 *Romans 1-8.* Vol. 38a of the *Word Biblical*
        Commentary. Dallas, TX: Word Books, Publisher.
Edersheim, Alfred
  1876 *Sketches of Jewish Social Life in the Days of Christ.*
        New York: Fleming H. Revell Company.
  1950 *The Temple: Its Ministry and Services.* Grand Rapids,
        MI: William B. Eerdmans Publishing Company.
Elefante, John, Dino Elefante, and Scott Springer
  1990 "We Need Jesus." On *Petra Praise 2: We Need Jesus*
        CD ROM. Uncle Pitts Music/Dayspring Music.
Elwell, Walter A., ed.
  1988 *Baker Encyclopedia of the Bible.* Vol. 2. Grand
        Rapids, MI: Baker Book House.
  1989 *Evangelical Commentary on the Bible.* Grand Rapids,
        MI: Baker Book House.
  1996 *Evangelical Dictionary of Biblical Theology.* Grand
        Rapids, MI: Baker Book House.
Engstrom, Ted
  1976 *The Making of a Christian Leader.* Grand Rapids, MI:
        Zondervan Publishing House.
Ervin, Howard M.
  1987 *Spirit Baptism: A Biblical Investigation.* Peabody,
        MA: Hendrickson Publishers.
Ferguson, Everett
  1993 *Backgrounds of Early Christianity.* 2nd edition.
        Grand Rapids, MI: William B. Eerdmans Publishing
        House.
Foster, Richard
  1992 *Prayer: Finding the Heart's True Home.* New York:
        HarperCollins Publishers.

Frangipane, Francis
1991 *The House of the Lord: God's Plan to Liberate Your City From Darkness.* Lake Mary, FL: Creation House.
Freedman, David N., ed.
1992 *The Anchor Bible Dictionary.* First edition. Vols. 1-3, 6. New York: Doubleday.
Gaebelein, Frank E., ed.
1976 *The Expositors Bible Commentary.* Vol. 10. Grand Rapids, MI: Zondervan Publishing House.
1981 *The Expositors Bible Commentary.* Vols. 9 and 12. Grand Rapids, MI: Zondervan Publishing House.
1984 *The Expositors Bible Commentary.* Vol. 8. Grand Rapids, MI: Grand Rapids, MI: Zondervan Publishing House.
1988 *The Expositors Bible Commentary.* Vol. 4. Grand Rapids, MI: Zondervan Publishing House.
1992 *The Expositors Bible Commentary.* Vol. 3. Grand Rapids, MI: Zondervan Publishing House.
Gilbrant, Thoralf, ed.
1986 *The Complete Biblical Library: New Testament.* Vols. 11-12, 15-16. Springfield, MO: World Library Press, Inc.
1986 *The Complete Biblical Library: New Testament.* Vol. 13. Springfield, MO: World Library Press, Inc.
1987 *The Complete Biblical Library: New Testament.* Vol. 14. Springfield, MO: World Library Press, Inc.
Giles, Kevin
1995 *What On Earth is the Church: An Exposition in New Testament Theology.* Downers Grove, IL: InterVarsity Press.
Gilliland, Dean S.
1998 *Pauline Theology and Mission Practice.* Eugene, OR: Wipf and Stock Publishers.
Glasser, Arthur F.
1989 *Kingdom and Mission.* Pasadena, CA: Fuller Theological Seminary.

Graham, William F.
  1953   *Peace With God*. Garden City, NY: Doubleday and
         Company.
Grenz, Stanley J.
  1994   *Theology for the Community of God*. Nashville, TN:
         Broadman and Holman Publishers.
  1996   *Created for Community: Connecting Christian Belief
         with Christian Living*. Wheaton, IL: Bridgepoint
         Book.
Gundry, Robert H.
  1994   *A Survey of the New Testament*. Third edition. Grand
         Rapids, MI: Zondervan Publishing House.
Hamman, A.
  1971   *Prayer in the New Testament*. Chicago, IL: Franciscan
         Herald Press.
Harper, Michael, ed.
  1978   *Bishop's Move*. London: Hodder and Stoughton.
Harris, R. Laird, Gleason L. Archer, Jr., and Bruce K Waltke,
  1980   eds. *Theological Wordbook of the Old Testament*. 2
         Vols. Chicago, IL: Moody Press.
Hart, Larry D.
  1999   *Truth Aflame: A Balanced Theology for Evangelicals
         and Charismatics*. Nashville, TN: Thomas Nelson
         Publishers.
Hawthorne, Gerald F., and Ralph P. Martin, eds.
  1993   *Dictionary of Paul and His Letters*. Downers Grove,
         IL: InterVarsity Press.
Hayford, Jack
  1987   *Worship His Majesty*. Dallas, TX: Word Publishing.
  1991   *Spirit-Filled Life Bible*. Nashville, TN: Thomas
         Nelson Publishers.
Iverson, Dick, and Larry Asplund
  1995   *Building Churches That Last*. Portland, OR: Bible
         Temple Publishing.

Jeremias, Joachim
  1969   *Jerusalem in the Time of Jesus: An Investigation into
          Economic and Social Conditions During the New
          Testament Period.* London: SCM Press Ltd.
Johnson, Luke T.
  1992   *The Acts of the Apostles.* Collegeville, MN: The
          Liturgical Press.
Keener, Craig
  1993   *The IVP Bible Background Commentary: New
          Testament.* Downers Grove, IL: InterVarsity Press.
Keith, Jennie
  1982   *Old People, New Lives.* Chicago, IL: The University
          of Chicago Press.
Kistemaker, Simon J.
  1990   *New Testament Commentary: Exposition of the Acts of
          the Apostles.* Grand Rapids, MI: Baker Book House.
Kittel, Gerhard, and Gerhard Friedrich, eds.
  1964   *The Theological Dictionary of the New Testament.*
          Vols. 1, 6-8. Grand Rapids, MI: William B. Eerdmans
          Publishing Company.
Kraus, C. Norman
  1993   *The Community of the Spirit: How the Church is in the
          World.* Revised edition. Scottdale, PA: Herald Press.
Küng, Hans
  1971   *The Church.* London: Search Press Ltd.
Ladd, George Eldon
  1959   *The Gospel of the Kingdom: Scriptural Studies in the
          Kingdom of God.* Grand Rapids, MI: William B.
          Eerdmans Publishing Company.
Landman, Isaac, ed.
  1941   *The Universal Jewish Encyclopedia.* Vol. 4. New
          York: The Universal Jewish Encyclopedia, Inc.
  1942   *The Universal Jewish Encyclopedia.* Vol. 8. New
          York: The Universal Jewish Encyclopedia, Inc.
  1943   *The Universal Jewish Encyclopedia.* Vol. 10. New
          York: The Universal Jewish Encyclopedia, Inc.

LaSor, William S., David A. Hubbard, and Frederic W. Bush
  1996 *Old Testament Survey.* Second edition. Grand Rapids,
       MI: William B. Eerdmans Publishing Company.
Latourette, Kenneth S.
  1975 *A History of Christianity: Beginnings to 1500.* Revised
       edition. Vol. 1. San Francisco CA: HarperCollins
       Publishers.
Laymon, Charles M., ed.
  1971 *The Interpreter's One-Volume Commentary on the
       Bible.* Nashville, TN: Abingdon Press.
Lea, Larry
  1987 *Could You Not Tarry One Hour?* Lake Mary, FL:
       Creation House.
Lee, Witness
  1985 *Life-Study of Acts.* First edition. Vol. 5. Anaheim,
       CA: Living Stream Ministry.
Lucado, Max
  1998 *Just Like Jesus.* Nashville, TN: Word Publishing.
Malherbe, Abraham J.
  1983 *Social Aspects of Early Christianity.* Second edition.
       Philadelphia, PA: Fortress Press.
Matthews, Victor H.
  1991 *Manners and Customs in the Bible.* Revised edition.
       Peabody, MA: Hendrickson Publishers.
Miller, Madeleine, and J. Lane Miller
  1973 *Harper's Bible Dictionary.* Eighth edition. New York:
       Harper and Row Publishers.
Mish, Frederick C., ed.
  1993 *Mirriam Webster's Collegiate Dictionary.* Tenth
       edition. Markham, ON: Thomas Allen and Son
       Limited.
Morris, Leon
  1991 *The First and Second Epistles to the Thessalonians.*
       Revised edition. Grand Rapids, MI: William B.
       Eerdmans Publishing Company.

1995   *The Gospel According to John.* Revised edition.
        Grand Rapids, MI: William B. Eerdmans Publishing
        Company.
Packer, J. I., Merrill C. Tenney, and William White Jr.
1995   *Nelson's Illustrated Encyclopedia of Bible Facts.*
        Nashville, TN: Thomas Nelson Publishers.
Pentecost, J. Dwight
1981   *The Words and Works of Jesus Christ: A Study of the
        Life of Christ.* Grand Rapids, MI: Zondervan
        Publishing House.
Richards, Lawrence O.
1985   *Expository Dictionary of Bible Words.* Grand Rapids,
        MI: Zondervan Publishing House.
Richards, Lawrence O., and Clyde Hoeldtke
1980   *Church Leadership: Following the Example of Jesus
        Christ.* Grand Rapids, MI: Zondervan Publishing
        House.
Richards, Lawrence O., and Gilbert Martin
1990   *Lay Ministry: Empowering the People of God.* Grand
        Rapids, MI: Zondervan Publishing House.
Robertson, A. T.
1930   *Word Pictures in the New Testament.* Vol. 3.
        Nashville, TN: Broadman Press.
Schaff, Philip
1985   *The Creeds of Christendom.* Vol. 2. Sixth edition.
        Revised by David S. Schaff. Grand Rapids, MI: Baker
        Book House.
Simeon, Charles
1956   *Expository Outlines on the Whole Bible.* Vol. 17.
        Grand Rapids, MI: Zondervan Publishing House.
Smith, David L.
1996   *All God's People: A Theology of the Church.*
        Wheaton, IL: Bridgepoint Book.
Snyder, Howard
1977   *The Community of the King.* Downers Grove, IL:
        InterVarsity Press.

Tenny, Merrill C.
  1965 *New Testament Times.* Grand Rapids, MI: William B.
        Eerdmans Publishing
        Company.
  1985 *New Testament Survey.* Revised edition. Grand
        Rapids, MI: William B. Eerdmans Publishing
        Company.
Tenney, Merrill C., ed.
  1975 *The Zondervan Pictorial Encyclopedia of the Bible.*
        Vol. 5. Grand Rapids, MI: Zondervan Publishing
        House.
Thirtle, James W.
  1915 *The Lord's Prayer: An Interpretation Critical and
        Expository.* London: Morgan and Scott.
Unity School of Christianity
  1962 *Metaphysical Bible Dictionary.* Lee's Summit, MO.
Van Engen, Charles E.
  1991 *God's Missionary People: Rethinking the Purpose of
        the Local Church.* Grand Rapids, MI: Baker Book
        House.
Vine, W. E.
  1952 *An Expository Dictionary of New Testament Words.*
        Nashville, TN: Thomas Nelson, Publishers.
Vine, W. E., Merrill Unger, and William White
  1985 *Vine's Expository Dictionary of Biblical Words.*
        Nashville, TN: Thomas Nelson Publishers.
Walvoord, John F., and Roy B. Zuck
  1983 *The Bible Knowledge Commentary: New Testament.*
        Wheaton, IL: Victor Books.
Warren, Rick
  1995 *The Purpose-Driven Church: Growth Without
        Compromising Your Message and Mission.* Grand
        Rapids, MI: Zondervan Publishing House.

Scripture Index

Subject Index

Aaron, 149, 187
abide, 42, 95, 164-167
abiding, 6, 164-166
Abimelech, 179
Abraham, 5, 16, 25, 36, 38, 58, 116, 175
accept, 11, 43, 46-47, 98, 101, 104, 157, 177
acceptance, 1, 4, 44, 89, 94, 97, 177
accepted, 1, 10, 27, 87, 89, 101, 126, 141, 168
acceptable, 27, 48, 149
Acts, 3, 13, 17, 25, 28-30, 40, 49-53, 55-61, 63, 72-73, 78-82, 85, 98, 106, 112, 118, 123, 125-128, 130-137, 139, 140-148, 151, 153-154, 159, 160-161, 166, 170
Adam, 33, 36, 86
adulterers, 25
adultery, 25-26
adulthood, 26
Africa, 16, 27
Agrippa II, 20
Alexander the Great, 8-9, 11, 14-15
Alexandria, 11, 17, 132
all believers, 21, 59, 84-85, 96, 120, 122, 148-151, 153-155, 158, 161, 171, 187
Almighty God, 93
Amidah, 71
Ananias, 29, 131, 146, 148
Andrew, 21, 30
anoint, 161
anointed, 3, 136, 146
anointing, 2, 153, 159, 171
Antioch, 17, 112, 142, 144-145, 153
Apollos, 112, 118, 143, 145

apostle
    John, 31, 108, 165
    Paul, 13, 54, 63, 82, 84, 96, 99, 111, 116, 119, 124, 137, 172
apostles, 8, 29-30, 49-52, 55, 58, 61, 63-64, 75, 79, 105, 112, 127-130, 132-133, 136, 139, 141, 143-144, 147, 155
Aquila, 118, 123, 143
Aramaic, 66, 79
Aristarchus, 56, 144
aristocracy, 20-23
Artaxerxes, 182
Artemis, 72
Asia, 16-17, 63, 70, 148
Asia Minor, 70
Athens, 8, 11, 15, 141
authority, 20, 50-51, 54, 99, 108, 113-114, 124-125, 128, 150, 152, 153, 179

Baal, 72
Babel, 57
Babylon, 8, 16, 36, 57
Babylonian, 15, 63, 181, 183
baptism, 3, 57, 62, 75, 82-88, 96-97, 126, 130, 153, 172, 188
baptized, 59, 75, 85-87, 96, 116, 130, 141, 143
Barnabas, 29, 98, 112, 130, 145, 147, 151, 153
barriers, 2, 17, 143
Baylonian Exile, 63, 181, 183
Beatitudes, 95
believers
    new, 81-82, 87, 97, 148, 161
Benjamin, 179-180
    tribe of, 178
Benjaminite's, 179-180

212

Greek Index

Author Index

Vita

Sheldon Orville Juell was born on April 19, 1962, in Assiniboia, Saskatchewan, Canada to Dr. Norman Douglas and Sharon Elaine Juell, the second of three children. He accepted the Lord Jesus Christ at the age of eight at Trossachs Gospel Camp. He was baptized in water at Maranatha Christian Centre in Regina, Saskatchewan in 1977. At the age of 26, he began his missionary journey by joining Youth With A Mission (YWAM) and shortly after was married to Ivone Maria Garcia Abdon Demetrio of Belem, Para, Brazil.

Sheldon began his theological training at Full Gospel Bible Institute in Eston, Saskatchewan where he majored in Pastoral Studies and graduated in April 1993. He then earned a Bachelor in Theology degree at Briercrest Bible College in Caronport, Saskatchewan in May 1994. After taking a year off to minister in Belem, Brazil, he earned a Master of Divinity at Oral Roberts University in Tulsa, Oklahoma in May 1998, and then moved to Pasadena, California where he completed the Master of Theology in Intercultural Studies at Fuller Theological Seminary. He is presently pursuing a Doctor of Philosophy in Intercultural Studies also at Fuller Theological Seminary. His future plans involve returning to Brazil to continue planting churches, teaching in Bible Colleges and Seminaries, and training Christian leaders.

Sheldon's wife, Ivone also majored in Pastoral Studies at Full Gospel Bible Institute and graduated in 1993 and completed her Bachelor of Theology degree at Briercrest Bible College in May 1994. She earned two Master of Arts degrees in the areas of Christian Counseling in May 1997, and Marriage and Family Therapy in May 1998 at Oral Roberts University. She is presently pursuing a Master of Arts in Theology and ultimately a Doctor of Philosophy in Clinical Psychology, specializing in Neuropsychology. Her plans are to return to Brazil and work as a Christian Psychologist.

Their ultimate plans are to start a Christian University in Belem, Brazil where they will seek to supplement the theological and missiological education of its students and other Christian leaders with appropriate psychological, sociological, and educational knowledge in an attempt to help alleviate human suffering and build healthier families, churches, and communities. This training will seek to equip each student with the knowledge and skills to take the gospel into all areas of society.

Sheldon and Ivone are presently members of Angelus Temple in Los Angeles, California. He teaches in the Angelus Institute of Ministry and The King's College at The Church On The Way in Van Nuys, California. He also teaches online courses for the Full Gospel Bible Institute in Eston, Saskatchewan, Canada.

To order copies or contact the author:

Present Address: Sheldon and Ivone Juell
(until 07/2003)   296 N. Oakland Ave. #7
Pasadena, CA 91101
Phone/Fax: (626) 405-8181
E-Mail: shelone@fuller.edu

Canadian Address: Sheldon and Ivone Juell
(Permanent)   c/o Dr. Norman and Sharon Juell
P. O. Box 1559
Assiniboia, SK   S0H 0B0
Phone: (306) 642-4931
Fax: (306) 642-5515
E-Mail: n.juell@sk.sympatico.ca